12 UNDENIABLE LAWS OF PRAYER

WHAT THE BIBLE SAYS THAT CAN EMPOWER YOU TO MANIFEST HEAVEN ON EARTH

BY: TIFFANY DOMENA

TABLE OF CONTENTS

PREFACE

Deuteronomy 28:1 says, "If you fully obey the LORD your God and carefully follow all his commands I give you today, the LORD your God will set you high above all the nations on earth." This book is not a treatise on positive thinking; though outlook does have a part. It's a book about faith interacting with the power of God. This book will not suggest that the imagination is the only necessity for answers, but it will tell you the role of visualization when seeking God. This book does not esteem that you are god or that you can create your own answers to prayer. It will not suggest that if you perform a deed that God will answer your prayers. This book requires your obedience and submission to the King of Kings, which for some, may be uncomfortable.

In every country, there is a philosophy about prayer: some must face a certain direction, some must sit, stand, or kneel. Some people speak in English, some french, some mandarin, and there are many other languages that are prayed. Some pray with the same commitment as they eat, others pray when tragedy strikes, and some have completely abandoned the idea of prayer. Many of the philosophies practiced throughout the world have only fractions of biblical basis, and only a small percentage of people get their desired results.

The Bible talks about the importance of prayer, and men (with astonishing legacies and stories) have been able to defend its truth with the testimony of their lives. Could prayer be the missing link that has stopped you from manifesting Heaven on Earth?

God is a person. He is not a human, but as a person does, He makes choices, He communicates, and He has a will. Therefore, we cannot exhaustively say or assure that any action of yours will guarantee an action from God UNLESS He has said it. In this book, we discuss how you can align yourself with the promises of God, and receive His blessings. We discuss the art and the science of prayer, so that you can finetune and grow your relationship with God.

Prayer can be likened to the foundation of a home. When the foundation is solid, winds, storms, earthquakes, or collision do not cause the house to fall. When the foundation is not solid (due to poor structure or being planted on bad soil), every storm, every wind, every earthquake, and every collision causes the house to shake; possibly even fall.

Prayer is communication with God, it gives you a firm foundation to build your life, and it increases in results as the relationship grows. As a result of prayer, the possibilities of your life are immense! This book will give you insight for how you can grow your relationship with God and tips from the Bible on how you can increase your effectiveness in prayer.

I want to congratulate you for getting this book and committing to transforming your life thru the art of prayer. This book is assured to be a benefit to anyone who desires to increase their connection with Heaven and manifest more than ever before. Prayer is a vital practice to understand. It affects every facet of your life, and can be the single key to your joy or sorrow, sickness or health, bondage or liberty. In Matthew 21:22, Jesus said, If you believe, you will receive whatever you ask for in prayer." This book will provide you with:

- 12 Laws for manifesting Heaven on Earth
- Illustrations that will reprogram your mind and teach you new ways to pray prayers that matter
- Advice for increasing your success in prayer
- A divine commission for increased openness while waiting on your answers

INTRODUCTION

Prayer has always been a practice that has surrounded me. In the US, prayer was comforting. In Iraq, prayer was a highly regarded ritual. In Africa, prayer induced miraculous signs. On an international scale, I saw people that regarded prayer and those that disregarded it. With such differing expectations of prayer, I became interested in how one can maximize their results from prayer.

Jesus told us that we should pray "Thy Kingdom come", so the Bible tells us that those that practice prayer should request and expect the manifestation of the Kingdom of God. With the biblical idea of Kingdom manifestation in mind, I began asking questions:

- If the perfect Kingdom of God can manifest when we pray, why aren't more people praying?

- Why doesn't everyone expect transformation when they pray?

- Why are prayer routines so different?

- Are prayers always answered?

- And many more

This book answers my questions and the questions of many others on the topic of prayer. It compiles groundbreaking research and experiences, so that you can manifest Heaven on Earth in your prayers.

May this book transform your prayer life!

-Tiffany Domena

CHAPTER ONE

MARRY THE HOLY SPIRIT

"God's desire is to not only have you experience His love, but to totally overwhelm you with His love. To have you experience it to overflowing. To have you sense, feel, taste, and touch His love for you. He really wants you to experience Him!"

– Linda Boone, *Intimate Life Lessons; developing the intimacy with God you already have.*

The Story Of Maxwell and Mariah

Mariah was married to a man of God named Maxwell. He loved her with all of his heart. They had three children, and appeared as a dream couple.

Behind close doors, Maxwell and Mariah were having small conflicts that were piling up. Despite her love for Maxwell and his love for her; they both would fail to uphold one another's desires. Mariah wanted to spend two or more hours with her husband daily. Her husband wanted to provide his wife with lots of amenities, so he had a difficult time meeting her quality time needs. He would wake up before sunrise to begin work and he would return after sundown. When he would return, he was tired and overwhelmed with preparation for the next day's work, so he did not make much time for his family. Mariah would get frustrated saying, "It seems that the children and I are not that important to you because you don't spend much time with us." He would say,

"I want a good future for you". The frustration between the two of them continued to increase; their intimate and playful affection turned into stern, stiff, disappointment. The kids rebelled because they desired more attention from mom and dad, but Mariah was so sad and her husband so busy that the kids did not get either of their attention. Before long, the kids were acting in an uproar, and Maxwell and Mariah were considering divorce.

Mariah had a wise friend named Portia that she decided to consult with. Portia had been happily married for 10 years and had a passion for making marriage work. Mariah cried, "It seems like Maxwell does not care. I make time for our marriage everyday, but he is so concerned about his business that he neglects me and the kids. I don't care as much about the amenities as I do about his time. I didn't get married so that I could be alone; chasing him around to give him breakfast, lunch, and dinner as he is tending to his clients. His temperament is so unstable because he is not getting proper nutrition or rest. He doesn't have time to make goals, grow his relationship with God, or plan for business advancement, so that he can stabilize the business and spend time with us. I feel like a single mother and I would prefer to be one rather than having more obligations with no benefit."

Portia said, "You were supposed to marry the Holy Spirit before you married a man. If your relationship with the Holy Spirit was stronger, you would not worry so much about earthly relationships. Do you have dates with the Holy Spirit? Do you talk to Him? Do you tell him good morning?"

"No", Mariah replied. "I desire my husband, and I wake up frustrated that he rolls out of bed without greeting me and rushes to work."

"Rather than focusing your attention on your husband, begin to focus on the Holy Spirit. Wake up desiring Him. Spend your date time with Him. He knows that you desire your husband and true love comes from Him. He is the third strand to your marriage chord. If your relationship with the Holy Spirit is as intimate (if not more) than your relationship with your children or your husband; all of your other affairs will reflect His favor and sovereignty."

Mariah began dressing up and dating the Holy Spirit. She would talk with Him. He would talk with her. He poured ideas into her and she would manifest them. She began to make money consistently and her husband did not have to work as much. The Holy Spirit taught her how to be a better wife and mother. Her kids became less disobedient. Her marriage was salvaged and her affairs flourished. Within 10 months, she went from non-moneymaking stay-at-home wife to an income that was upwards of $10,000.00 monthly.

Treat The Holy Spirit As Your Perfect Spouse

Your closest relationships (to include your spouse) will never reach perfection. Relationships cannot be fulfilling without love. Because we are fallen beings, love requires continual effort. When we try to love, we reach limits. How do you talk to your friend? How do you talk with your spouse? God desires your utmost intimacy. He has created relationships with people as an image for you to see and understand the limitless possibilities of being in relationship with someone who has access to all, knows all, has the power to give all, and wants to hear from you regularly.

As Mariah did, she loved her husband, but she was disgruntled by the fact that he did not invest time into their marriage. Maybe for you, time is not the condition to your love. Maybe gifts may be the condition to your love, maybe services, touch, words, or respect. We all have conditions to our love, and when we connect to the Holy Spirit, we can transcend those conditions. He tells you what to do, where to go, or what not to do. He is your guide.

Prayer is communication with God. Prayer is not passive, but it is interdependent; where we participate in the manifesting process by faith. God is three parts as you are: Father, Son, and Holy Spirit. You are Spirit, Soul (cognition and intuition), and physical.

Just as a baby develops the cognition and ability to bend their fingers. They learn to connect their thoughts with the physical reaction. Their body develops so they learn that if I can bend my fingers with my thoughts, then, I can bend my elbow with my thoughts, and the correlations develops to more difficult tasks. As an adult, you are still learning the limitless physical abilities that you have when you combine persistence, willpower, and action.

Prayer opens the possibilities so much more because thru prayer you can transcend physical boundaries and laws by invoking the agent (God) that connects all things seen and unseen. Rather than connecting your thoughts and the transmission of them thru your spinal chord to your limbs, in prayer you are connecting your words of faith spoken to the King of Heaven with physical and spiritual reactions. Learn the science of prayer.

As Sir Isaac Newton said regarding motion, "Every action has an equal and opposite reaction". The Bible says that prayer surpasses the laws of motion by not only granting an equal reaction, but surpassing the initial reaction many times over. Matthew 21:22 says, "If you believe, you will receive whatever you ask for in prayer." Your investment in prayer time yields higher returns than any investment fund, working compensations, book royalties, real estate returns, relationships, and anything else that one can imagine. You invest time in prayer and in return you can receive ANYTHING. Heaven offers the GREATEST investment plan with the least effort. You do not have to have anything aside from the time that has already been invested by God in you. Why sweat when you have that type of access? Why worry when you are in communion with the single shareholder of the galaxy?

If you want things to manifest on Earth, you must grow your faith thru Bible Intake and prayer. There is no effective prayer without the Holy Spirit. He is your advocate and the medium that forms the atoms and molecules that you have spoken with your biblically congruent words to manifest Heavenly things on Earth. Therefore John 14:26 says:

"However, the helper, the Holy Spirit, whom the Father will send in my name, will teach you everything. He will remind you of everything that I have ever told you. "

Prayer is not monotonous or mechanical. Effective praying is birthed in a relationship with the Holy Spirit. This is something that flows through you to the Father without having to work anything up; prayer that naturally flows spontaneously from your heart without rehearsal because you are in talking terms with Heaven through the Holy Spirit. You and the Holy Spirit are friends.

Be elated by His presence

To cultivate the Holy Spirit's friendship, you have to conscious-ly develop an excitement for His presence. When your spouse knows that you are always excited and enthusiastic about meeting him or her, they don't spend extra hours away from you. If you have friends that you get excited to see, then you understand the excitement that should be present in your relationship with the Holy Spirit.

I can remember deploying with the US Air Force to Iraq in June 2010. In August 2010, I met my husband. I was deployed as a security guard and my husband needed to be escorted in cer-tain areas of the military installation. He had been in Iraq for more than two years by the time that we met, and had highly anticipated marriage. We meshed immediately. I loved him and he loved me and our friendship grew from this genuine spiritual connection. After two months of spending 4 to 6 hours together daily, my deployment was over, and I left Iraq in September 2010.

When we last saw each other in Iraq, we vowed to stay in touch. My husband had to find new employment, I missed sleep, and we abandoned other meetings and gatherings just so that we could talk on the phone. After one year of being separated, my husband had planned our wedding, and bought a ticket for my son and I to accompany him in Ghana . The anticipation of seeing him and getting married to him streamed excitement thru my whole body! The days could not go by fast enough. My thoughts and dreams were overwhelmed by thoughts of what I would do when I saw him. Our conversations were concentrated on what will happen when we get together. Our friends, families, and co-workers were excited for us because we had told everybody (even passer-bys on the street).

Your excitement about the presence of the Holy Spirit should surpass my excitement to see my husband. When His presence comes, the feeling overwhelms your senses beyond any physical activity that can take place on the Earth. The results of the Holy Spirit's visitation far surpass the results of anyone or anything else. Natural disasters cannot cause the same impact as the Holy Spirit. When the Holy Spirit arrives, transformation is sure to take place. With your spouse or a friend, you may expect to tell them something exciting or hear some exciting information. With the Holy Spirit, you can be excited about transformation in your life and the lives of others. Talking with the Holy Spirit enables you. The Holy Spirit is a person; treat Him greater than the most loving couple treats their spouse on their honeymoon.

Invite Him within you

In her book, Intimate Life Lessons, Linda Boone says, ""Soaking" seems like a crazy word in an intimacy book. Yet that is exactly what you want to do in your relational time with Him, you want to "soak in and soak up" His presence, "soak in and soak up" His love." Jesus said when the Holy Spirit comes, He shall be in you. And if you being evil know how to give good gifts to your children, how much more shall the Heavenly Father give the Holy Spirit to those who ask of Him (Luke 11:13). Just say, "Holy Spirit, come", and He will sure come. In that way, you invite Him into your innermost being.

Put Him in your schedule. It is only people and events that are important to us that we put in our schedules and make plans for. In the same way, if we want to continue in friendship with the Holy Spirit, we would have to make daily plans to make time with

Him. Be sure of this: when you make time for the Holy Spirit, He will make time to visit you.

Budget for things that can increase your relationship with Him. I cannot personally recount the many times, I've had to make adjustments in my finances for my spouse. That was even before we got married, let alone now that we are married. And why was I doing all that? It was such that our relationship can get better. This is true of the Holy Spirit, He feels His importance in your life with the way you treat Him. You know that you are loved by the way that you are treated. Treat God with the esteem and value that He deserves. If you feel that He deserves it all; invest your life into manifesting His will for your life.

Make a budget for books, videos, conferences, and conventions that will enhance and increase your relationship with Him. He knows when your heart is after Him. For action speaks louder than words.

Charm Him

A friend of mine told me a story. He said:

"I remember, the first time I met my spouse. I didn't know we would be in a relationship, and I REALLY had not guessed that we would get married. I went from a mountain where I went to pray, then I visited her older brother who was living in a nearby city near the mountain's base.

I was taken in the spirit of worship, and as such, it was my custom to unconsciously sing and worship the Lord. I had no idea that as I was worshipping, a woman was attracted to my voice.

The rest is history. I later found out that it was those songs and particularly my voice that first got into her before I ever said a word. I charmed her unknowingly with my voice."

Similar to the way that my friend attracted his wife, you can charm the Holy Spirit, and have Him stay with you all the time. We can do this effectively thru acts of service, spending quality time, giving gifts, songs of praise, living a pleasing life, and words of affirmation.

'Assuredly, I say to you, inasmuch as you did it to one of the least of these My brethren, you did it to Me. (Matthew 25:40). Your acts of kindness to your neighbors can influence your relationship with the Holy Spirit. In those acts, you are doing what He loves to do. He is finding expression through you. Your waking up in the morning and saying "Good morning Holy Spirit, is an act that would show your interest in communion with Him.

Spend quality time with the Holy Spirit. In my book 12 Undeniable Laws of Marriage, I talked about how to identify quality time. I likened time to diamonds. With diamonds, they are difficult to find. Quality diamonds have minimal scratches, impurities, and discoloration. When a high-quality diamond is found, it is secured and separated from harmful possibilities.

Quality time is just as quality diamonds; it is hard to find and secure. Life presents many choices, and time can be invested into many things. Quality time has no adulteration; it is focused and without distraction. Quality time must be protected by good scheduling and time management. It must be protected by communication, and using your "no" power when other opportunities arise. You must say, "No. I cannot participate in that now. This is my time with the Holy Spirit." You will find that by consecrating time for the development of your relationship with the Holy Spirit, you will have immense spiritual growth.

Relationships are always nurtured and groomed through gifts. The relationship with the Holy Spirit is the same. The greatest gifts we can give to the Holy Spirit is to add others who desire a relationship with Him. A soul winner is never void of His presence.

How would you describe a child who always does the opposite of what the parents want; always violating orders and living in disobedience? Disobedient children are a disgrace to their parents. To maintain the friendship of the Holy Spirit one should live a life that is consistent with the revealed word of God, otherwise we would be living in His displeasure.

The more affirmative you are with words (particularly in declaring the word of God over your life, circumstances and situations) the more you come into close relationship with the Holy Spirit. The Spirit and the Word are one. Therefore, the Holy Spirit will have full expression and right of way in an atmosphere where the word is believed and affirmed with all sincerity. We can create a faith-filled enabling environment of the Spirit by a bold proclamation of the word of God.

Summary

Marry The Holy Spirit: Treat Him As Your Perfect Spouse

Be elated by His presence

Invite Him within you

Put Him in your schedule

Budget for things that can increase your relationship with Him

Charm him with acts of service, quality time, giving gifts, living a life that pleases Him, and words of affirmation

CHAPTER TWO

LEARN THE ART AND SCIENCE

"Is prayer your steering wheel or your spare tire?...There are no 'if's' in God's world. And no places that are safer than other places. The center of His will is our only safety - let us pray that we may always know it!"

— Corrie ten Boom

Thomas Edison is one of the most influential inventors to have ever lived. He developed the idea that certain metals can pick up on certain currencies and transmit it to our devices which would create electricity. He added to that idea that power centers can be built that can transmit electricity into millions of homes. All offspring of the idea of electricity have collectively changed the world. Today, most households across the world use the power of electricity to bring light to their homes and power their devices.

Similar to what Thomas Edison did to discover electricity is what can be done to manifest Heavenly things thru prayer: experimentation. Prayer works similar to science. Prayer is a stimuli that causes reactions. Just as electricity is unseen, but by the flip of the switch, lights turn on, so also by the words spoken in prayer, miracles manifest. Prayer is a science because it can be studied, learned, and applied.

Prayer is an art because it requires skill. Similar to a painting that is made beautiful with an eye-catching subject, color, lines, shadows, texture, and surface. Prayer is made complete and productive thru the articulation of words along with praise, worship, quoting of the Bible, and the most intimate cries and pleas of the soul. The skill of prayer can be acquired by experience, study, or observation. Like every other occupation requiring knowledge and training, prayer does too! There are skills to effective praying that have to be learned.

You must become acquainted with the study (the science) and the art (practice) of prayer to enhance your results. Any study that cannot be applied or is not applied is not study at all but a waste of time. Prayer is not something to just study and not apply, but your investment in it is much greater than any other education you could ever attain.

The Story Of Molly and Her Unanswered Prayers

Molly is a Christian. She spends 20 minutes per day praying to God. The typical format of her prayers is problem, plea, and "Amen". Typically, she prays as she is driving home from work in her car. One day on her way from work, she told God:

"Dear God. I never know if you hear me. I cannot see the results. I tell you all my problems and request that you change them, but I do not see the results. I am going to try this prayer thing once more and if I do not see results, I am going to stop. Here we go…

God, you saw my co-worker speaking negatively to me today just like they do everyday. Why can't you stuff her mouth with something that disables her to speak that way to me? I hate hearing her speak. Her voice is annoying to me, but it is even worse that she is saying negative things towards me. Please shut her mouth.

God, I want a nicer car. It is 2015 and I am still driving a 2013. Why can't you bless me like you blessed my boss? I want more money! I want a 2015 more than this 2013. Why can't you give it to me?

God, I do not want drama when I go home. I had a bad attitude yesterday, and my husband was frustrated when I left home. Please make him forget what happened yesterday, so I can have peace.

If you hear me, I want to see my answers today. Amen."

When Molly got home and unlocked the door, her dog had chewed her Bible and left it laying face down on the floor. Upset, she ran to it and picked it up. When she flipped it right side up and looked at the damaged pages, a scripture stuck out to her which said:

"Shout for joy to the Lord, all the earth. Worship the Lord with gladness; come before him with joyful songs. Know that the Lord is God. It is he who made us, and we are his; we are his people, the sheep of his pasture. Enter his gates with thanksgiving and his courts with praise; give thanks to him and praise his name. For the Lord is good and his love endures forever; his faithfulness continues through all generations."[1]

Molly felt like a dagger had pierced her heart and she wept before God. She realized that her prayers had always been focused

---

[1] Psalms 100

on herself rather than respecting the King of Kings. She realized that she never said, "Thank you for what I have", but rather she complained to God daily about what she wanted and what she didn't have. As she cried, she said

"Thank you Father that you have spared my life. I have presented myself completely blemished before you time and time again. I have never expressed gratitude for the things you have done as your word says. David said that we should enter Heaven's gates with Thanksgiving and I thank you Father for hearing my prayer. I know that despite my complaining and the sound of a bitter and never satisfied child ringing before you, you heard me, and instructed me on how I can improve my relationship with you. I vow to you Father that today and forevermore I will reverence you as my King. I will make the name of your son known and great rather than concerning myself with my own worries, I will invite your Kingdom to inhabit every aspect of my life. I love you, my Father and my King, and I pray all these things in Jesus name. Amen"

Molly spent the remainder her evening singing songs of praise. She sung:

"You are Alpha and Omega! I worship you, my Lord. You are worthy to be praised."

Prayer can be improved

The fact that prayer is an art makes for the possibilities of its being improved. If you have been praying, you can get better at it and the results you get will prove that. Improvement comes by learning and doing. Like Molly, you may be a Christian who prays problems and thoughts in prayer and have never heard about the kind of prayer called "praying the word." But the moment you study and learn that art, and go into practicing it, you can be sure that your prayer would have improved and become more effective. The answers that you would start having would prove the authenticity of that new art and practice.

God desires that His Kingdom be manifested on Earth as it is in Heaven. For this reason, Jesus instructed us to pray, "Thine Kingdom come on Earth as it is in Heaven". Prior to the fall, man walked alongside God in the Garden of Eden. We know that the Garden of Eden had no death, shame, no evil or wrongdoing, and it had abundance. God wants to restore this abundance to the Earth, but you must align completely with His will, which is beyond you. You cannot be selfish in prayer because God is not selfish. He wants all of mankind to be positively affected. How can you expand your view to bless others with the answers to your prayers? Molly prayed that her co-worker's mouth would be stuffed, but her prayer was only for her personal satisfaction. If she had prayed that the hatred, greed, and evildoing be removed from her workplace, the prayer would have transcended her own selfishness and positively affected many more people in her workplace.

God has no desire to remove our ability to choose. You can choose to do good or bad things. I can choose to do good or bad things. As a result of our choices, we have a lot of chaos in our world: robbery, theft, terrorism, war, and so on. God does not desire to remove anyone's option to make good or bad choices, but He does desire to remove the evil from the world. My choices will affect more than just myself, and so do yours. Our choices can transcend our generation and effect people many generations after us. Thru prayer, we can gain strength to overcome difficult opposition, so that we can be a greater positive effect on others. We can break bigger barriers than one person's bad choices and we can remove the root of the evil in the world (fruits of the flesh and submission to temptation).

The results of prayer can be measured. A wise man once said that it is not so much as to the results he gets in answer to prayers as much as the changes that happens in him when he prays. Prayer transforms the outside and inside of you as you pray.

Many times the answer to the prayer is not tangible, therefore, we overlook the manifestation of the answer. When you pray, you may receive ideas, you may receive relationships, character changes, you may receive wisdom, a word of faith, prophecy, or a physical response. You must have open eyes to the varying portals that God uses to pour your answers. Whether the answer was given in physical form or implanted in the mind, we can measure our prayers by the results that we get.

Prayer Results can be seen

God is hearing the prayers of His people. He transmits the cries of one child to his other that can solve the problem. How many people struggled with international communication? How many people had loved ones across the planet separated from them? How many wanted to hear from or see their loved ones? God heard and knew their pain. He sent an idea to many people who collectively created phones, internet, international calling plans, boats, airplanes, and many more ideas were birthed as a result of a King who answers international petitions. Creation is a testimony of the power of God. Inventions and man-made creations are a testimony that God hears our problems and plants ideas to solve them.

Be Authoritative In The Creative Process

There was a man that worked with the elephants at the zoo. Day in and day out, he would go out and give instructions: "Sit", "Walk", "Lay". The elephants did not respond to anything that he would say. For onlookers, they thought the zookeeper was crazy, they would laugh, and the veterinarians said that the elephants were deaf. The zookeeper did not believe anything that he was told. He remembered going out on the safari and spotting the elephants as babies. He told them to come to him when they were in danger of being attacked by a lion and in that moment, they ran to him. The zookeeper held onto that memory and believed that the elephants could hear. After one whole year of repetition, saying the same commands, and demonstrating what needed to be done when the command was spoken, the zookeeper was able to witness the elephants doing what he said. He learned the volume that appeals to the elephants, the distance that he should stand when speaking, the rewards to give them when they are obedient. He learned the secret sauce that transformed his relationship with the elephants and earned him their loyalty and obedience.

Similar to the story of the zookeeper, we have a role in prayer. Prayer is a creative process and our responsibility is to hold strong in faith. Despite the appearance that could have planted doubt about whether the elephants could or could not hear, the zookeeper held strongly onto his memory of the elephants when they heard him before. Similarly, despite the appearance of opposition, you must hold onto the words that have been spoken from God.

Increase your Bible intake, so that by repetition, you can be reminded of the promises of God.

When I think of creativity in the art of prayer, the picture that comes to my mind is that of Abraham when He stood before the Lord in intercession for the cities of Sodom and Gomorrah. In Genesis 18:20-32 Abraham had a conversation with God. The Bible says:

Then the Lord said, "The outcry against Sodom and Gomorrah is so great and their sin so grievous that I will go down and see if what they have done is as bad as the outcry that has reached me. If not, I will know."

The men turned away and went toward Sodom, but Abraham remained standing before the Lord. Then Abraham approached him and said: "Will you sweep away the righteous with the wicked? What if there are fifty righteous people in the city? Will you really sweep it away and not spare the place for the sake of the fifty righteous people in it? Far be it from you to do such a thing—to kill the righteous with the wicked, treating the righteous and the wicked alike.Far be it from you! Will not the Judge of all the earth do right?"

The Lord said, "If I find fifty righteous people in the city of Sodom, I will spare the whole place for their sake."

Then Abraham spoke up again: "Now that I have been so bold as to speak to the Lord, though I am nothing but dust and ashes, what if the number of the righteous is five less than fifty? Will you destroy the whole city for lack of five people?"

"If I find forty-five there," he said, "I will not destroy it."

Once again he spoke to him, "What if only forty are found there?"

He said, "For the sake of forty, I will not do it."

Then he said, "May the Lord not be angry, but let me speak. What if only thirty can be found there?"

He answered, "I will not do it if I find thirty there."

Abraham said, "Now that I have been so bold as to speak to the Lord, what if only twenty can be found there?"

He said, "For the sake of twenty, I will not destroy it."

Then he said, "May the Lord not be angry, but let me speak just once more. What if only ten can be found there?"

He answered, "For the sake of ten, I will not destroy it."

I want you to see the process that was involved in Abraham's prayer. You see how Abraham made his case before the Lord from one level of bargaining to another. Gradually, like an artist Abraham created his art, look at how skilful and adept he was at it. He negotiated with God basically inquiring about His level of loyalty to people that uphold His commands.

Prayer is like a painting, singing, or playing sports. It requires skills that can be acquired by experience, study, or observation. Similar to the zookeeper, he had to learn the volume, distance, and rewards that the elephants wanted to receive. You also must learn how to please the royal Recipient of your prayers. You see we can liken prayer to the artist who crafts his painting. Skills and creativity go into prayer.

Understand The Fulfillment That Comes From Prayer

Another fact I want to bring out is the excitement and fulfillment that prayer brings. Despite the odds, the zookeeper diligently went out, tended to the elephants, and spoke the verbal commands. He never lost his zeal to spend time with them even when they were not adhering to his words. Let us look at the example of Abraham again. Did you see the sense of awe mixed with excitement with which He approached the Lord? And oh, what fulfillment came on Abraham when He had fully expressed himself before the Lord.

There is great fulfillment that comes from knowing that you have had quality time with your Maker. You come out completely overwhelmed by the feelings of romance, and knowing that you have been heard beyond what you have said, but thoroughly understanding what you mean. When you have touched Heaven, you come out satisfied, fulfilled, convinced, relaxed, and knowing that everything has been settled.

Prayer prevails over willpower, physical laws, and every earthly opposition (even death). There is great potency and far reaching power in prayer. Prayer knows no barrier; it is like an intercontinental ballistic missile that reaches into the continent of the living and of the dead; across time and eternity. Prayer defies every law and order of the universe. The law of gravity cannot work on prayer. I should liken prayer to the realm of God, where all things are possible, where nothing is limiting or inhibiting, where time, life or death is not a factor.

"Lazarus, come forth!", Jesus called. The realm of the dead (beyond time), heard it and responded.

I want you to understand that the Word in faith is like your paint brush. The zookeeper held onto the memory of when the elephants did hear. Abraham knew that God loved the righteous and He held onto the idea of His love. The Word of God is that memory that you must hold onto. When thoughts of doubt arise, you must say, "No! I remember what your word says, and this is not in agreement with that". A prayer in faith is the substance of creation. Prayer and The Word of God go together. Prayer is actually taking God's word back to Him, holding forth his word back to Him as if to say, "Lord you said it , now do it". An effective prayer life is one that is founded and grounded on the word of God. In praying, we actually pray God's word back to Him.

Take a careful look at the ministry of Jesus, and you can conclude that it was a ministry of the "Word." To the blind, Jesus would say, "Receive your sight." To the lame, He would say, "Rise up and walk." To the sinner, He would say, "your sins are forgiven you." And to the leper, even after touching him, would say, "Be clean." Words! Words! Words!

It was with faith-filled words that Jesus did His ministry; the same word by which God created the Heavens and the earth. It is with those same words that we have power with God in creation. With words, we create our world.

You must understand that the results you get in prayer stem from your commitment. You need to see artist when they are working on album, night after night, day after day, they spend time unending in the studio until they come out with a master copy of that piece. The result is always dependent on their commitment; how much time they invest into making the piece. It was said in the gospel accounts of Jesus that He spent all nights in prayer to God. He invested time in prayer. Little did we wonder that He had all time answers to His prayers? (See Luke 6:12).

God is not a Puppetmaster!

Brenda is a Christian woman. She has been a greeter at her church for 14 years. Her pattern is to spend Saturday nights working at the local strip club, change her clothes (or put some on), and go to church.

When Brenda talks about God, she depicts him as a puppetmaster. She says, "He is up there pulling the strings, making me do things that I do not want to do, so I don't see the purpose in talking to Him too much." Brenda does not feel the need to pray because she feels that the conclusion is already firmly in place, so she allows life to drift and make decisions for her.

Some people think that God is static. They claim that the God of the Bible is silent or distant, but they simply have not build a relationship with him. Some people think that life is chosen for them and are unaware of their authority in creating their life picture. The Bible tells us that God is the beginning and the end, but it also tells us that we have a role in choosing the course of our lives. Proverbs 16:1 says, "The plans of the heart belong to man, but the answer of the tongue is from the Lord." Many things in the middle have not been chosen, but rather are left to man as God's ambassadors on the Earth. He is aware of your options and the possible outcomes, but God has truly created us in His image, therefore, we are permitted to create or fail to fulfill our destinies.

The problem of the world is that the authority that has been bestowed on man has been abused. From the fall of man on, man has surrendered his territory to tempting things, and reaped detrimental consequences as a result. For this reason, Deuteronomy 30:19-20 says, "I call heaven and earth to witness against you today, that I have set before you life and death, blessing and curse. Therefore choose life, that you and your offspring may live, loving the Lord your God, obeying his voice and holding fast to him, for he is your life and length of days, that you may dwell in the land that the Lord swore to your fathers, to Abraham, to Isaac, and to Jacob, to give them."

Be authoritative in your prayer time, understand that you are a part of the creative process, and your choices are painted into your life picture. God created the Earth and He is aware of all of the possibilities of your choices, but He allows you the sovereign role of making decisions and dealing with their consequences. Prayer is your chance to tap into divine thought, and make decisions that can stimulate good results; rather than making decisions that negatively affect you and those around you.

Summary

- Prayer is an art and a science
- It can be improved
- Results can be measured
- Results can be seen
- Prayer is a creative process
- Prayer is like a painting, singing, or playing sports
- It is exciting and fulfilling

- It prevails over willpower, physical laws, and every earthly opposition (even death)
- The Word in faith is like your paint brush. It is the substance of creation
- The results stem from your commitment

CHAPTER THREE

GROW INSIDE AND OUTSIDE INTO YOUR ANSWERS

"The function of prayer is not to influence God, but rather to change the nature of the one who prays."

— Søren Kierkegaard

The Story Of Jyrus

There was a young boy names Jyrus. He had an astounding imagination. He would tell his parents that when he grows up, he would be the most famous bodybuilder in the world. Jyrus started conditioning at age four in preparation for his dream. His parents were happy for Jyrus to have such a large dream, but inside, they did not know how his dream would be possible since he only had one arm.

When his mother took him to gyms where bodybuilders condition, they would always say, "His frame is too small to ever be a bodybuilder. Besides, how could he ever lift heavy enough weights to condition with one arm?"

Jyrus never lost sight of his dream. He engineered his own equipment to accommodate his physical impairment. At age 18, he had been conditioning for 14 years. There was no league for men without all of their limbs, so Jyrus decided to create one. He attracted people from all over the world who wanted to compete and add their skills to the bodybuilding niche, but never had the chance due to physical impairments.

Jyrus became madly successful and highly respected in the bodybuilding circle. His physical training equipment line for the physically impaired became a multimillion dollar company. When the traditional bodybuilding league saw his capabilities with one arm, they asked for him to join their league and be a spokesperson to show bodybuilders all over the world what perseverance means. Jyrus broke many world records, won world championships, and was recognized with three honorary doctorates degrees for his role in the bodybuilding industry.

Be Persistent In Prayer

Typically, there are time lags between the time we pray and when the answers materialize. For Jyrus, he had a dream of his adulthood from when he was four-years old. In times like that of Jyrus, you may have to grow into the answers of your prayers for years before it can manifest. Jyrus had to do muscle conditioning and build an attitude of perseverance to defy the insults and other difficult opposition that he would encounter to pursue his dream.

In other miraculous instances, your answers may materialize in milliseconds or less. The waiting time is as important as the prayer itself. It is during the time lag that many lose heart and give up on their prayers. Let me tell you, it matters what and how you do after you have prayed. This is because faith is a necessary condition for answered prayer.

You're probably wondering, "What am I supposed to do during

those times when my prayer is still in its maturity process?" Grow! Inside and outside, grow! This is the time to soak yourself in the word of God. The Word of God is a forever settled word. It stays and stands stable when those feelings of excitement and exhilaration are no longer there. It is at this time you persevere as said in Hebrews 6:10-12. It says:

"For God is not unjust to forget your work and labor of love which you have shown toward His name, in that you have ministered to the saints, and do minister. And we desire that each one of you show the same diligence to the full assurance of hope until the end, that you do not become sluggish, but imitate those who through faith and patience inherit the promises."

At these waiting moments, God expects us to grow inside and outside into the answers of our prayers. Did you know that the reason why we have to wait for some answers is because God is waiting for us to grow the ability to manage the answer when it comes? God will never give us something that we don't have the capacity to handle. So what are we supposed to do? Grow into the answers of our prayers!

Life Changes Occur to Answer Prayer

I have seen people that their lives took a dramatic change at the instance of an answered prayer. They gain calmness, certainty and assurance of life I have seen people awestricken-with reverence and a holy loving fear, when they finally had the answers in their hands.

Sometimes the answers to prayer will remove unproductive people from your life, renew character, change reputations, restore self-esteem, relocate you, or other changes may occur. You may have to be submissive to the inkling to make dramatic changes in order to walk into the answer to your prayer. Prayer will make changes happen; many times uncomfortable changes, but shifts must take place for growth. Just like intense pressure and poking must take place to tenderize meat, so also does intensity in decision-making and grace soften the heart.

Life Trials May Come Before Your Answer

Life trials may come to test your preparedness for the answer. As surely as the Lord lives, the devil will give you a fight for that prayer you are expecting answers to. He will stir up the winds against you, and send trials and tribulations, but know this, those tests are there to strengthen you, to prepare you for the answers to those prayers. I believe the apostle James speaks clearly about this in James 1:2-4: "My brethren, count it all joy when you fall into various trials, knowing that the testing of your faith produces patience. But let patience have its perfect work, that you may be perfect and complete, lacking nothing."

Character Changes Occur to Answer Prayer

Marcus was a man in his mid-twenties. He came from an impoverished family. Marcus had a bad habit of lying. He wanted to pastor a church, so he did well in school, and applied for a scholarship to go to ministry school. When he was in his Master of Divinity program, he stole $10.00 from his roommate. When his roommate asked him, "Marcus, have you seen my $10.00?" Marcus said, "Naw, man! Look under your bed!". When Marcus had left the room, his roommate found the $10.00 in his night-stand drawer.

When he returned to his room, his roommate (also a seminary student) confronted Marcus. He said, "Marcus, you and I both have a heart to serve God. We both love helping people, and we both want to lead people into doing what is right." Marcus looked, nodding in agreement. His roommate continued, "In order for us to lead people into right action, we must perform right action". Marcus nodded. "Marcus, I found my $10.00 in your nightstand drawer. I still honor your heart for God, but your lying has to stop for your ministry to be successful". Marcus contemplated. He knew that his roommate was telling him the truth. He thought about the roots of his lying and how he was taught to lie by his parents. They would tell him to lie to avoid bill collectors, he would lie on their behalves to deter the pastors, he would lie on their behalves to keep them out of jail, and his own lying had become habitual. He told his roommate, "It would help me for you to hold me accountable to change, and pray with me. I need God to transform my character and make me whole. I should not feel like I have to lie or take what is not mine, but the act of lying has been planted so deep that I did it without thinking about it". His roommate said, "We'll pray about this day and night, and I will point out to you whenever I notice you saying something that is not true, then we will stop and pray for forgiveness and redemption". Marcus prayed with his roommate and he built a new habit of truth.

Character improvement is an ongoing necessity for us to manifest our purpose in life. When someone points out to you a character flaw, you must be open to talking to God, finding the root, and uprooting the evil from your life. Sometimes, character changes are a necessity prior to the answer to your prayer materializing. Like Marcus who wanted to pastor a congregation, sometimes the character flaws that we have would repel good results from manifesting when we have received the answer to our prayers. Be open to transforming your character so that you can be in harmony with the answer to your prayers.

It is very easy to get offended when someone points out an imperfection in you, but you must maintain the humility enough to allow sin to be identified and corrected. When you allow emotions to control and offense to set in, it expands the hold of that poor behavior in your life. Let it go!

Changes may be perceived as painful

I remember a friend testifying of his experience with receiving his answer to prayer, he said:

"In prayer, I was asked to leave my steady, successful life and move into ministry. I knew God was talking to me but the cost seemed high. I had to obey. It was going to require that I relocate from the city I was living to another: a new city and tribe in Africa that was entirely different from my own. But I had to obey and go, regardless of how painful it seemed at first.

But the end of it is the glory and the testimony that has long graced my obedience. What I thought was going to set me back, actually brought about my lifting. The ministry grew very quickly: new members were joining weekly, people's lives were being transformed, and what I perceived as pain has actually turned to be a gain. I could have never achieved the level of fulfillment that I feel from mentoring so many people by sticking with my previous job or pursuing anything else."

Sometimes the radical actions that we must take may appear to be painful or we may know or feel that others (our friends, families, co-workers, etc.) will oppose our decisions, but Jesus required radical behavior in Luke 9:23-26 when he said:

"Whoever wants to be my disciple must deny themselves and take up their cross daily and follow me. For whoever wants to save their life will lose it, but whoever loses their life for me will save it. What good is it for someone to gain the whole world, and yet lose or forfeit their very self? Whoever is ashamed of me and my words, the Son of Man will be ashamed of them when he comes in his glory and in the glory of the Father and of the holy angels."

The cross was the symbol of a painful execution that was used to punish criminals and those who oppose the Roman government. In the US, a comparable symbol would be the electric chair that kills criminals thru intense electric voltage. Whatever is your symbol of retribution, Jesus said that we should deny ourselves, take it up, and follow him. He did not say be so passive and word-conscious that you avoid offending everyone while following him. Rather, he said that even to the point of physical death, he wants us to be so radical for the spread of the gospel and the manifestation of our particular assignments within that spread that we face as fierce an opposer as death. We may face hate, jealousy, outbursts of anger, sexual immorality, and many other things that oppose the will of God. When we face this opposition whether we are facing it thru our own personal struggle or by pointing out this evil to free someone else, the reactions range in intensity and opposition towards you. Prayer adds heat to the breakthrough.

The process of uprooting means that the root must be identified and removed, which is painful in most instances. Do not shy away from removing the root because you see or perceive pain; pull it up for God's glory; His way! Add grace when needed, use wisdom always, and intensify prayer as wisdom guides. Prayer opens your access to your Heavenly allies and you need them because intensity hints that the kingdom of darkness has made their stance on the issue, therefore, you must also alert the armies of Heaven to defend your case.

Know that growth inside and outside is mandatory to have a heart prepared for the answers of God. He does not place you in authority of or enlarge territories for people who are not prepared to handle them. When you begin to pray about life matters and Kingdom matters, be prepared for change to take place.

Transformation comes from spending quality time with God in the place of prayer

The Bible recorded a story that perfectly illustrates what could happen to a person who takes time out with the Lord very often. It is the story of Moses documented in Exodus chapter 34. Read the entire chapter for greater understanding, but for the sake of our discussion here, we will read verse 30-34 which says:

"Then the LORD said to Moses, "Write these words, for according to the tenor of these words I have made a covenant with you and with Israel." So he was there with the LORD forty days and forty nights; he neither ate bread nor drank water. And He wrote on the tablets the words of the covenant, the Ten Commandments. Now it was so, when Moses came down from Mount Sinai (and the two tablets of the Testimony were in Moses' hand when he came down from the mountain), that Moses did not know that the skin of his face shone while he talked with Him. So when Aaron and all the children of Israel saw Moses, behold, the skin of his face shone, and they were afraid to come near him."

It says that Moses was there with the Lord, and when he returned, his face glowed, so the people could not look on Moses' face! The transformation that happened in Moses still occurs today! Most of the time the transformation is not a physical alteration as Moses' was, but the spiritual transformation causes this same resistance in the spiritual realm. The kingdom of darkness cannot look in the direction of a person that has spent dedicated time in prayer and fasting (as Moses did) with God.

Though the physical glow may not be as common or as apparent (where people cannot look at the person), but there is a glow and assurance that graces the person that spends time in prayer. Obstacles, changes, attitudes, or other commonly frazzling events do not cause an obstruction of their view of the power of God. Opposition ceases to sway a person that knows their power in prayer.

It was said of Stephen in Acts 6:15 that all who sat in the council, looking steadfastly at him, saw his face as the face of an angel. There was a glow on the face of Stephen that could not be mistaken.

That of Moses and Stephen were physical (that still happens today), but yours might not be that way. Nevertheless, a change still happens particularly on the inside when you pray.

For instance, I discovered in my prayer life that the more I pray, the less I talk and the keener my mind becomes. I have noticed for my husband that his intellect comes alive particularly when he prays in tongues. Though I have not been given the gift of speaking in unknown tongues as this present moment, I am aware of the power of using the gifts that God has given us spoken of in 1 Corinthians 12:8-10 (the message of wisdom, the message of knowledge, faith, gifts of healing, miraculous powers, prophecy, distinguishing between spirits, speaking in different kinds of tongues,and interpretation of tongues) to add additional intimacy when in the presence of God. With love being present first, each of the gifts can bring added intimacy and can increase the transformation that takes place. The gifts that God has given as tools can bring vast transformation when they are used properly. That's change! That's transformation!

The deeply rooted must surface

When you pray, things that you did not know were in you will start showing up. Some things that are deeply imbedded (possibly even appearing natural), that are not apparent to you, begin to surface. Prayer makes apparent the things in your life that must be removed for your forward-movement. Some of the things that might surface in you will even surprise you. Sometimes, those things might not even be in you, but can be in your family, your city, your house of residence, your church, your government, or even the world at large. Things that the eyes and mind can never or would never have seen or imagined.

Confrontation surfaces

Another area that things will begin to surface is the area of confrontation. I mean the devil will give it to you. I find out that any time I take special time out to pray and seek God, the devil will always look like he is let loose in full force. Hell will just break loose. I know that such times of confrontation are not the time to stop praying but the time to fire on. The mistakes most believers make at this level is to quit praying, and this should not be so.

For me, I take every confrontation from hell as a backhanded compliment from Satan, as if to say, "You are disturbing me." I like to take back my territory from the devil, you know! I remove his authority to wreak havoc in my life and the lives of those in my view. He doesn't like that.

I particularly welcome those confrontations. And true to my nature, I would fight until I see the end of it.

Results manifest

I like to see the end of things. And do you know the end of such confrontation? Paul gave it to us in the following words:

"Yet in all these things we are more than conquerors through Him who loved you." (Romans 8:37)

And, Jesus even says it better:

"These things I have spoken to you, that in Me you may have peace. In the world you will have tribulation; but be of good cheer, I have overcome the world." (John 16:33)

We know the end; victory for us and defeat for he who was defeated eternally by Jesus Christ, the Son of God. Sure enough, the transformation process has taken place; the deeply rooted has surfaced and has been dealt with; the confrontation has come and gone; now as surely as the Lord lives, the result will show. It is a natural law; the day follows the night, the rains follows the cloud, and the victory follows the faith battle.

Summary

- We must be willing to grow inside and outside into the answers of our prayers
- Life changes occur to answer prayer
- Life trials may come to test our preparedness for the answer
- Character changes occur to answer prayer
- Changes may be perceived as painful
- We must expect the prayer transformation process before answers are birthed
- The deeply rooted must surface
- Confrontation surfaces
- Results manifest

CHAPTER FOUR

GIVE AND RECEIVE PRAYER

"God can deliver anyone from anything at any time. He doesn't need any help. Yet He invites us to be part of His great work through prayer. Never underestimate the effects of intercessory prayer lifted for our deliverance. Never underestimate the effect of prayer for others. If we don't intercede for one another, we miss opportunities to see His deliverance and to thank Him for His faithfulness. I call this God's profit-sharing plan. When we pray for one another, we share the blessings when His deliverance comes because we've been personally involved."

— Beth Moore (Believing God Day by Day: Growing Your Faith All Year Long)

Matthew was an astronaut. Alot of studies and new discoveries were taking place in space. As an astronaut, he submitted himself to solidifying the studies, proving hypothesis, and exploring space. His job pulled him away from his family quite frequently. He would fly out on missions quarterly for at least one week.

He had a daughter named Victoria that was experiencing her pubescent ages. She began to grow breast, she started to menstruate, and became curious about how to dress to accent her new figure well. Victoria began to dress based on what she saw on television: short shorts, short skirts, tight shirts, shoulders exposed, cleavage when possible, and her back out. Her mother thought of her new dressing style as a fad. She would say, "I am sure she will only dress like that for a season, but I will let her work it out on her own."

Matthew did not agree with the way Victoria began to dress, she was a beautiful girl with a beautiful figure, and he was sure that men could not keep their eyes or hands off of her if she were too close. He did not want her to experience the perversion of men and he wanted her to enjoy the intimacy of marriage, so he told her mom, "You cannot let her buy things like that! She is beautiful and I want her to know it, but she does not have to show it. Men are out there that will abuse her beauty and innocence, and dressing like that makes her a target."

One day, when her dad was on a space mission, Victoria was given permission to go to the mall with her friends. She wore some of her most provocative clothes, but her mom said, "It is up to her. She has to learn on her own". Some older guys (appearing in their late 30's) followed Victoria and her friends thru the mall, they bought them milkshakes, and Victoria and her friends thought they were so kind. Within one hour of drinking the milkshakes, Victoria and her friends felt very dizzy and delusional. The guys stayed with them and eventually escorted them from the mall to a nearby hotel. Victoria and each of her friends were used to fulfill sexual favors without being conscious of the ordeal. The next day, they woke up naked, in a puddle of blood, in pain, and with no recollection of what happened. The girls sobbed. They did not know how to contact their parents or what to tell them.

Matthew had a very eerie feeling about his family. On his mission, he began to pray:

"God, I am unsure why I feel so frazzled about my family. I

know of your immense power. I know that you understand circumstances that are beyond my knowledge or my reach. I need you to protect my family. Send your angels to post guard around them. Secure them wherever they are, and let your power be known to them now".

Victoria said to her friends, "We have got to get out of here! We do not know if those guys are coming back. Let's catch the city transit and go to my house. My mom can help us figure things out". They left, went to Victoria's house and consulted with her mom who initiated the medical, spiritual, and legal process to receive the help that they needed.

Intercessory Prayer Can Reach Places Nothing Else Can

Spiritual laws exists and are constant, regardless of whether you practice them on Earth, in prayer, or in outer space. Giving and receiving is one of such laws that exists in all realms, and not only in the realm of finances. We can make prayer such a spiritual proposition: giving and receiving prayers to and from the people around us. Jesus said in His commentary on giving and receiving in Luke 6:38 "Give, and it will be given to you: good measure, pressed down, shaken together, and running over will be put into your bosom. For with the same measure that you use, it will be measured back to you." It is important for us to know that Jesus was not only talking about money when He made that comment, He was looking at the picture of giving as a whole. If a man wants a child, he gives the wife semen and she would in return give him a child. She receives the semen and he receives the child; they have both given and have both received. When a man needs watermelon, he gives the soil a seed of watermelon and in return he gets watermelon back. They have given and have both received.

In the case of Victoria, her dad interceded for her, and she received the comfort and inspiration to get help in her situation. Even though her dad was not aware of the details of her situation, he was obedient to the inkling that he got about his family, and interceded on their behalves.

Request intercession

"…pray for us, that the word of the Lord may run *swiftly* and be glorified, just as *it is* with you, and that we may be delivered from unreasonable and wicked men; for not all have faith. (2 Thessalonians 3:1-2) Again Paul asked in Ephesians 6:18-20 that he be prayed for, "that utterance may be given him, that he may open my mouth boldly to make known the mystery of the gospel, for which he was an ambassador in chains; that in it he may speak boldly, as he ought to speak."

Paul presented a scriptural example of one asking and requesting intercession. We should follow in Paul's footstep. For he himself said, follow and imitate me as I follow and imitate Christ.

Intercession can be helpful to present barriers that you may be unaware of. For example, Victoria was naively experiencing her pubescent phases and exploring dressing options. Her father was aware of potential dangers that can happen as a result of some of the people in her area being exposed to her beauty. Sometimes, you may make naive decisions out of curiosity, making a firm stance for change, or as a result of following something that you have seen others do. When you request others to intercede for you, you plant the idea within others to pray for your wellbeing.

Others have a different perspective on your life. They may see a tragedy before you do. They may see a blessing that you do not. It is vital for you to tap into the power of unity and the power of several different viewpoints under one God who can combine several petitions, and arrange them to work together for His glory. Ask for prayers!

Intercede for others

Today, many people face opposition as a result of the choices of their forefathers and those that have preceded them in combination with their own choices. When you combine bad choices with childrearing, mentorship, or simply having onlookers; many generations can have spiritual trauma because of the bad choices of one person. Let me tell you Brittany's story, she is the perfect illustration of how bad choices of one person can affect many.

Brittany was the daughter of an unequally yoked couple. Her parents were married at 18 and 19. Her mother, Gina, was the daughter of a pastor and was raised in the church, but because of some poor choices that her father made, at age 15 she vowed never to step a foot into a church building again. Gina's father, Pastor Watkins, had an affair with the church choir director when Gina was 14. This really affected the family because they had idolized their father and viewed him as the epitome of what a man should be. When he committed this wrongful act, they generalized all Christians to be hypocrites because they began to see that all people commit wrongful acts.

Gina went on to date Romeo. Romeo's family was largely a part of a local gang. They were always attempting to defend their reputation and fought large groups of people at least once weekly for reasons such as "he looked at me wrong", "she shouldn't have said that", or "I just didn't like him".

When Gina and Romeo married, they incorporated habits from both of their families: drugs, fighting, adultery, and out-bursts of anger became common appearances within their marriage. Brittany and her siblings had seen her mom beat by her dad, her dad sleep with her mom's sister, many wild parties, many fights, and the list goes on.

When Brittany was 20, Gina decided to give her life to God. She began making demands for her family to change, but the habits and choices that she had made had infiltrated her children's behavior and become even more heavily apparent than the proceeding generations.

Gina learned of her authority in Christ and began interceding for her family. Thru her intercession, her family began to be more open to observing Gina's perspective, and Brittany was the first to give her life to Christ. Brittany began a catalyst movement in her community and became very successful, sharing the message of Christ on the radios, on television, and speaking all over the world. Her family chose to invest in a relationship with Christ because they saw the transformation of Gina and Brittany, and their family became an example for others in their community and across the globe.

Don't Underestimate The Power Of God Because Someone Falls To Temptation

Many have pushed God out of the creative and innovative business. Like Gina did with her dad, many people have placed an expectation for perfection in man, and become astonished when someone commits wrongful deeds. We all know that it's true that men in leadership and elsewhere have committed many wrongful deeds, and the Bible does emphasize that church leaders should uphold a certain standard. However, some people gossip saying, "Did you see what Pastor (so and so) did?"; rather than understanding that when someone has been approached by the kingdom of darkness, they have been studied prior to tempting, and they know weaknesses that transcend generations. They are highly qualified opposition! On their resumes, they have caused your father, your father's father, and many more to fall, therefore, intercession is your singular hope for prevailing enemy territories against evil. You need to pray for your leaders because they are leading many people, therefore, they are an increased target because of their level of influence.

Do you see how many people fell because of Pastor Watkins' act? I only shared the impact within his family, but many more people were witnesses of what happened and the negative impact that it had on the family. Many in the congregation turned away, many in the family shunned God and instructed others to do the same. The kingdom of darkness wants to "kill many birds with one stone". Therefore, we must pray for our leaders (spiritual, governmental, moral, and by whatever other forms of appointment). God releases His power on the Earth when we open the door for Him. Therefore, prayer is a critical tool that we can use for massive enemy destruction. Revelations 3:20 says:

"Here I am! I stand at the door and knock. If anyone hears my voice and opens the door, I will come in and eat with that person, and they with me."

I exhort first of all that ... intercessions ... be made for all men, for kings and all who are in authority, that we may lead a quiet and peaceable life in all godliness and reverence. (1 Timothy 2:1-2) Now that you have received, it is time to also give. Give in intercession for all people. Give in intercession for Kings, Presidents, Prime Ministers, and all who are in authority.

Make intercession a business of your life. You can only win people that you pray for. Take on a person in church or in your neighborhood who is not saved or sick or having trouble with his marriage and intercede for that person until you see the desired result. We don't have to wait for the Holy Spirit to particularly lead us into interceding for a particular person, places or things, if that happens, fine, but if not; don't wait! Just take on that lady or gentleman who is living in sin and pray her through to repentance.

I know of people with immense power through intercession. I know of people who are nation changers through intercession. I know of people who determine and influence the destinies of nations because they stood in the gap. What about Moses who prevented God from destroying the nation of Israel because he interceded. It was said that the queen of Scotland feared the prayer of John Knox more than her entire army. Then it was their time, but now; this is our time. This is your call and this is my call. Will you intercede for someone today?

Summary

- Give and Receive

- Request intercession

- Intercede for others

CHAPTER FIVE

VISUALIZE YOUR ANSWERS AND BE GRATEFUL FOR YOUR MILESTONES

"We have to pray with our eyes on God, not on the difficulties."

— Oswald Chambers

The Story Of Johanna and Family

It was Christmas, and Johanna had just experienced the most horrific day of her life. As she sat crying, she was overwhelmed with vivid flashbacks that seemed to drive her deeper and deeper into a worse state of depression.

On Christmas Eve, Johanna, her husband Jacob, and her two young boys, Jerry, age 7, and Joshua, age 11 had spent the evening wrapping presents, baking, and playing family games. Around 11 o'clock, they all fell asleep, and within two hours, Johanna woke up to thick clouds of smoke. Her husband jumped up and stormed out of the bedroom door saying, "I am going to get the boys. You go ahead out the window!" She followed her husband's instructions and exited the window. It took her awhile to get to ground level because her bedroom was three stories high, so it was about one hour before she reached onlookers to query about whether they had seen her family.

When the firemen arrived, she screamed panicking, "My husband and my sons are inside! Please go and save them!". They pulled their firehose and raised their ladder to try to reach her family. She said, "My boys were sleeping in the room on the second story, the window second from the right, and when we awoke to the fire, my husband went to save them. Please hurry and get my family out of the fire!" she cried.

The fire fighters stormed into the room that Johanna had told them about. The fire was escalating in intensity and smoke was seeping from the window. One firefighter came out, and another went in. This rotation happened for about 20 minutes. Then, they lowered the ladder and began to heavily spray the house with their firehose.

The Fire Chief came over to Johanna and said:

"Hello. My name is Chief Ward. I am the fire chief of the Summit County Fire Department. The firefighters have done their best to find your family inside of the flames, but only burnt remains were found. We tried to call out to see if anyone was alive inside, and unfortunately, no one was found alive inside of the house."

Johanna began to screech and scream in bitter anguish. She described the pain as "worse than someone pulling out my teeth and entirely cutting thru my genitals without anesthesia". She was taken to a mental hospital because she showed signs of suicidal ideation. She would say, "My family was the epitome of what I wanted in life, and I have lost them. What do I have to be grateful for now?"

A paralyzes woman named Terri began visiting Johanna. She

was paralyzed from the neck down. She was able to empathize with her because she lost her ability to move in a tragic car accident where she too lost her family. She told Johanna:

"I do not feel what you feel, but I can relate to what you feel right now. My story is very similar, and the pain was hard for me to endure. What changed my life is when God gave me His peace and altered the way that I think. Some of this is within your control because your mind is playing tapes that you can stop. You can invite God and His angels to help you change the momentum of the thoughts roaming thru your mind. You must change the picture in your mind. I used to re-imagine the image of the tragedy and ask myself, 'Why couldn't I go too?' or 'Why did this have to happen to them?', but when I realized how I can be closer to them now than ever before, it helped to relieve my pain. I began asking God to show me how to live past this tragedy, and I began using the legacies of my family to help other people. Today, I have started four foundations that empower others.

My husband was passionate about helping entrepreneurs who are starting from nothing to get funding and grow a successful business, so I started a foundation that does that in his honor. More than 20,000 people have been touched by his story and his life thru that foundation. My daughter was passionate about little girls whose parents could not afford nice toys, so I have started a foundation in her honor that has given away more than one million toys to young girls. My son was interested in young boys learning how to engineer and build things, so I have started a foundation that has taught over 50,000 young boys engineering and building skills. My family is very much remembered, and their legacy lives on thru the lives of millions of people today. My new image has changed from a picture of my family eating dinner and playing with my children's toys together to touching lives thru their passions. I push to touch lives because I understand that more than anything else, that is what we were placed here to do, and I know that because of Jesus Christ, I will see my family soon.

Johanna, you can change the image of your family too. You can take the wealth from the grave that the kingdom of darkness may think that they won from taking your family at such an early age. Pick up their legacies and use them to transform the world. Change your focus from the past (which is gone) to the future (which is yet to be)."

Johanna thought on what Terri told her, and she said, "Thank you because what you have said has given me hope".

Learn to visualize good in your future

Your mental picture solidified by God determines your actual future. Proverbs 19:21 says, "Many are the plans in a person's heart, but it is the Lord's purpose that prevails." As Terri presented, depression and joy can be controlled based on how we answer the question, "Where am I going?" and "How do I live past my hardships?". To visualize is to imagine, conceive of, or see in one's mind. It is a mental picture of something that is invisible or abstract. Johanna saw the past, which was gone; it was now invisible. Terri saw the future that is not yet here, and is also invisible. Both of them had experienced extreme tragedy, but because of the picture and their responses to the tragedy, one lives with peace and joy, while the lives in anguish.

At times like Johanna's, it may be difficult to see or understand the good in a circumstance, but despite our feelings, the Bible tells us to give thanks. When you seek God and ask, He can show you how to live beyond your situation and how you can reach your maximum potential now. The process of receiving begins by seeing in your mind the answers to your prayer, "as far as your eyes can see." Regarding visualization, Jesus said:

"The eye is the lamp of the body. If your eyes are healthy, your whole body will be full of light. But if your eyes are unhealthy, your whole body will be full of darkness. If then the light within you is darkness, how great is that darkness!"

At times it is a struggle to see past the obstacles. Sometimes, you must put increased effort into the filtering of your mind. You must outweigh your intake with good. Bible intake, affirmative music, stories of overcomers, etc. In these instances, where we have to self-discipline to persevere past the torment, Paul said:

Do you not know that in a race all the runners run, but only one gets the prize? Run in such a way as to get the prize. Everyone who competes in the games goes into strict training. They do it to get a crown that will not last, but we do it to get a crown that will last forever. Therefore I do not run like someone running aimlessly; I do not fight like a boxer beating the air. No, I strike a blow to my body and make it my slave so that after I have preached to others, I myself will not be disqualified for the prize. (1 Corinthians 9:24-27)

Then in doing this, we should never give up even when the answer to our prayers has not yet become physical. You see, in the law of the spirit, you don't have to have the manifestation in your hand before you know it's yours. It becomes yours first by seeing it in your spirit. After Terri told Johanna the testimony of her life, Johanna was able to see a different future for herself, and for the hope, she said, "Thank you". Your hope comes from God, and for this, you should give thanks.

There are two influences that increase your ability to create: 1. Your imagination or ideas, and (2) Your faith. When you have these two ingredients and they are consistent with the Kingdom laws and promises, you are assured to receive your answers. Hold on to the picture until you have the physical manifestation!

Summary

- Practice Thanksgiving
- Be grateful for answers and milestones
- Be grateful for the imaged vision
- Vision means that the creation has already taken place in the Spirit
- Meditate on the vision and the promises
- Visualize the answers
- Persist even when your answer has not yet become physical

CHAPTER SIX

USE DIFFERENT PRAYER POSTURES

"So the very beginning of godliness, the very beginning of transformation in our lives and in our society, begins with our posture before God.

— R.C. Sproul (The Prayer of the Lord)

The Story Of Brandon, the Dreamer

Brandon was a student in a boarding school in Ghana. His parents had sent him from his home in uptown New York City to boarding school in Ghana to give him a different perspective on life. As they forecasted, life was completely different.

When students did something wrong, rather than receive a pink slip, after school suspension, or a phone call home, students were spanked with a paddle in front of everyone. Their grooming habits were inspected (some things daily and some things weekly). Instructors would make sure that nails were clipped weekly, hair was kept neat, clothes were washed, and sleeping areas were intact. Daily, students were checked to ensure that shirts were tucked in, belts were securely fastened, socks were neat, everyone was implementing practices to grow their relationships with God, and students were timely.

Brandon had never been in an environment quite so structured. The students and teachers that were in his previous schools were very relaxed and most were disrespectful, but in boarding school, students did not come close to disrespect.

In his school in New York, Brandon was being considered to be drafted for the NBA. In boarding school overseas, it was unheard of to be drafted into professional basketball. Brandon really wanted the opportunity to be a professional basketball player, so in his prayer time, he would bow to his knees and pray to God asking for the chance to be considered for professional Basketball.

In his senior year in high school, another student named, Dante enrolled in the school from California. Brandon and Dante became very close and they were very competitive in Basketball. In the third semester (one semester before school was out), Dante's father came to visit them in boarding school. He told them that he had been tasked with drafting players for the Sacramento Kings. He said that it would be a breach of ethics if he were to draft either of them because of the circumstances, but he would give them an opportunity to show their talent to others who would be drafting for the NBA. Brandon fell prostrate and said, "Thank you God, for you have answered my prayer!"

Prayer Postures Have Meaning

The Bible shows many examples of prayer warriors using different prayer postures to add emphasis in their prayers. There are several prayer postures that are part of both the Old and the New Testament culture.

There is a correlation between the physical disposition and the spiritual disposition. A person who is overweight, that appears to have a buildup of dirt in the crevices of their skin and tartar buildup on their mouth with areas of browning on the teeth can be understood beyond their physical composure. A person who is very thin with scratches on his wrist, and tattoos about death on his neck can be understood beyond the physical dimension. Your physical body makes statements that reflect the status of your spirit. You can see virtuous character thru cleanliness, the physical stature, and the willingness to maintain your temporal home.

Similarly, you can use your body to show honor to someone or something by bowing, kneeling, laying prostrate, or raising the hands in a position of surrender. On the contrary, you can show dishonor by rolling the eyes, making distracting noises, or stomping the feet in anger.

Body language is a form of communication amongst man, and it is also useful in prayer. Prayer postures are not required to communicate to God, but they give added expression to the attitudes of our hearts. Some prayer postures make us more vulnerable; we may not have the same ability to defend ourselves. Prayer postures can signify humility as you abandon other people's thoughts of you to communicate a message before God.

Laying Prostrate Before God

Regarding lying prostrate before God, iblp.org says, "No position symbolizes humility better than being on our faces before God. This position of prayer demonstrates the beatitude of being poor in spirit. When Jesus described Himself, He said he was *meek and lowly in heart*" (Matthew 11:29.)"

This particular prayer posture is not peculiar to people who have seen the awesome holiness of the Lord. The twenty four elders in Heaven do this every day, proclaiming God's holiness. It is a prayer posture that relates the holiness of the almighty. No one sees the holiness of God and still stands up straight, he must bow with his face to the ground.

In Numbers 20:6-7, we see a picture of Moses and Aaron bowing down with their faces to the ground at the instance of the presence and glory of the Lord. The Bible says:

"So Moses and Aaron went from the presence of the assembly to the door of the tabernacle of meeting, and they fell on their faces. And the glory of the LORD appeared to them. Then the LORD spoke to Moses, saying,"

You see, the moment they fell on their faces before the Lord at the door of the tabernacle of meeting, the Glory, presence of the Lord appeared and God spoke. The posture was a unity of spiritual and physical disposition. They laid prostrate reflecting a genuine reverence and awe. Do you see what we miss when we don't practice this posture of prayer?

When we lay prostrate before God, we recognize:

• His power

When Elijah was showing the power of God in comparison to all of the other gods, he had built an altar, and had four large jars of water poured on the wood. The rest of the story is in 1 Kings 18:36-40. It says:

At the time of sacrifice, the prophet Elijah stepped forward and prayed: "LORD, the God of Abraham, Isaac and Israel, let it be known today that you are God in Israel and that I am your servant and have done all these things at your command. Answer me, Lord, answer me, so these people will know that you, Lord, are God, and that you are turning their hearts back again." Then the fire of the Lord fell and burned up the sacrifice, the wood, the stones and the soil, and also licked up the water in the trench. When all the people saw this, they fell prostrate and cried, "The Lord—he is God! The Lord—he is God!" Then Elijah commanded them, "Seize the prophets of Baal. Don't let anyone get away!" They seized them, and Elijah had them brought down to the Kishon Valley and slaughtered there.

- The awe of the presence of holiness

When Daniel saw a vision that he did not understand, God commanded the angel Gabriel to interpret the vision to him. Daniel 8:16-18 says:

"And I heard a man's voice from the Ulai calling, "Gabriel, tell this man the meaning of the vision." As he came near the place where I was standing, I was terrified and fell prostrate. "Son of man," he said to me, "understand that the vision concerns the time of the end." While he was speaking to me, I was in a deep sleep, with my face to the ground. Then he touched me and raised me to my feet."

- Our need for His mercy and grace

When the Israelites had built the golden calf and worshipped it, God became very angry, and said that He would destroy those who had forsaken Him. Moses interceded for them saying, "I lay prostrate before the Lord those forty days and forty nights because the Lord had said he would destroy you."

Kneeling Before God

Many churches exercise the use of kneeling as a routine way to pray. Kneeling is the physical position on the knees. This position is a symbol of the heart that honors God and understands His sovereignty and superiority to man. The Bible gives several examples of those who exercise kneeling as a prayer posture.

Kneeling can be used to show gratitude and express praise. It shows an attitude of reverence and submission to the Lord. God said in Isaiah 45:23: "I have sworn by Myself; The word has gone out of My mouth *in* righteousness, And shall not return, That to Me every knee shall bow, Every tongue shall take an oath. Someday whether we like it or not we will all have to bow our knees before the Lord. I think we better get used to it now such that it becomes a natural thing with us before God would compel us to doing it.

We see in the life of Daniel, that kneeling was a major practice in the Jewish religious worship system. It has not changed today. Three times every day according to the customs of the Jews is to pray, we see Daniel taking that posture in prayer. The miraculous deliverance that greeted his courage is proof that His prayers were not a waste of time. (See Daniel 6:10)

When the people of Israel had completed the building of the temple of God, Solomon gathered them, and dedicated the temple before them. 1 Kings 8:54 says, "When Solomon had finished all these prayers and supplications to the LORD, he rose from before the altar of the LORD, where he had been kneeling with his hands spread out toward Heaven."

King David instructed us to kneel in worship. We can ward off the kingdom of darkness in complete submission to God; kneeling and praying. Psalms 95:6 says, "Come, let us bow down in worship, let us kneel before the LORD our Maker"

Bowing

Again, we see the Eliezer in Genesis 24:26, bowing down his head in worship to the Lord who has granted him Godspeed as he went to get a wife for Isaac his master's son. So bowing is a prayer and worship posture that we must cultivate.

Bowing is one of the few prayer postures that God has specifically given instructions about. It is a position which says to Him, "You are the only God that I worship". To the children of Israel He said in Deuteronomy 5:6-10 "I *am* the LORD your God who brought you out of the land of Egypt, out of the house of bondage. ' You shall have no other gods before Me. ' You shall not make for yourself a carved image -- any likeness *of anything* that *is* in Heaven above, or that *is* in the earth beneath, or that *is* in the water under the earth; you shall not bow down to them nor serve them. For I, the LORD your God, *am* a jealous God, visiting the iniquity of the fathers upon the children to the third and fourth *generations* of those who hate Me, but showing mercy to thousands, to those who love Me and keep My commandments."

You see to God, bowing is key and central to worship and walking with Him. It is a statement of reverence and alliance. In bowing, we are not only praying but worshipping simultaneously. Bowing is where Satan has a problem with God. He also wants humans to bow and worship him. Be careful who you bow before!

Hands raised

Lives can be restored or taken away thru the hands. When we clench the hand we can pack a harmful punch or we can help someone to break free. When our hands are opened, we show our emptiness and desire for filling. In 1 Timothy 2:8, Paul says, "I desire therefore that the men pray everywhere, lifting up holy hands, without wrath and doubting;". When criminals are cornered, the police scream out, "Put your hands up?" Police ask suspects to raise their hands above their heads to show that they are carrying no weapon and have no intent to fight back. When your hands are lifted, you are showing vulnerability, and making known that you have relinquished the idea of defense. Your are saying, "I give up. I have no intent of opposing your will". You are surrendering.

When you raise your open hands, you could be saying, "Pick me up God. I need more of you. I need your filling". When you raise your hands with a closed fist, you could be saying, "I am holding onto you God. I will not let go. I receive what you have for me".

Standing

In 1 Kings 8:22, we see Solomon standing before the altar of the Lord, spreading His hands toward Heaven. He held this posture before God and the people of his kingdom as he dedicated the temple of God. The Bible says that "Solomon stood before the Lord."

When Abraham interceded for the cities of Sodom and Gomorrah, in Genesis 18:22-23, the Bible says:

"Then the men turned away from there and went toward Sodom, but Abraham still stood before the LORD. And Abraham came near and said, "Would You also destroy the righteous with the wicked?"

When you stand before God, you are representing your authority in the hierarchy. You understand that the kingdom of darkness is under your feet, and you stand relinquishing shame, guilt, or anything else that would cause you to hide from God. Standing before God says, "Here I am God. I come before you boldly".

Sitting

In 2 Samuel 7:18, we see King David introducing another prayer posture. The Bible says: "Then King David went in and sat before the LORD; and he said: "Who *am* I, O Lord GOD? And what is my house, that You have brought me this far?"

Sitting is a position of relaxation. After a lot of physical activity, sitting is usually a relief. When we sit before God, we are attentive and awaiting His peace.

Walking

When you walk with someone, it is a sign of agreement: you have a common destination or common stops along the way. God desires to walk with us. He wants us to align our destination to His abundant Kingdom; void of sorrow, pain, struggle, sickness, death, or any other turmoil. He desires to guide us thru life, but we have choices to make daily to stay harmonious with Him.

In Genesis 3:6-9, we see that God walked alongside Adam and Eve until they had done wrong and allowed their lust, guilt, and shame to take the away from walking in the perfect peace of God. The scripture says:

When the woman saw that the fruit of the tree was good for food and pleasing to the eye, and also desirable for gaining wisdom, she took some and ate it. She also gave some to her husband, who was with her, and he ate it. Then the eyes of both of them were opened, and they realized they were naked; so they sewed fig leaves together and made coverings for themselves. Then the man and his wife heard the sound of the LORD God as he was walking in the garden in the cool of the day, and they hid from the LORD God among the trees of the garden. But the LORD God called to the man, "Where are you?"

We have the opportunity to walk with God daily; it is a great privilege! Similar to walking with a human, when you walk with God, your lines of communication are open, you are within range to hear His voice, you can recognize His deeds, when He sends you a blessing, and He is willing to open His abundance when you have a close relationship with Him.

Have you ever seen the husband or the boyfriend who surprises his wife with a gift in the mail? When she opens the present and asks, "Who is this from?", how does that make him feel? Horrible!

Daily God sends you customized presents; suitable to your specific need and circumstance. Most people do not identify who has sent them the present. When you are walking with God, you know, no one else could or would do the things that God will.

In Micah chapter 6:8, we see God talking to the children of Israel regarding walking with Him. It says:

"He has shown you, O man, what *is* good; And what does the LORD require of you But to do justly, To love mercy, And to walk humbly with your God?"

It is all about understanding certain truths, practicing them consistently, and inculcating them into our everyday life as style and art. Prayer postures can assist you in communicating with God, so be open to express yourself to Him with every part of your being.

Summary

- Exercise the use of different prayer postures to communicate with God
- Standing as spoken of in 1 Kings 8:22
- Hands raised as spoken of in 1 Timothy 2:8
- Sitting as spoken of in 2 Samuel 7:18
- Kneeling as spoken of in Dan 6:10
- Bowing as spoken of in Gen 24:26
- Face down as spoken of in Numbers 20:6
- Walking as spoken of in Micah 6:8

CHAPTER SEVEN

CYCLE THRU DIFFERENT PHASES AND ENTER INTO THE HOLY OF HOLIES

"We can never know who or what we are till we know at least something of what God is."

— A.W. Tozer

The Story Of Larry, The Businessman

Larry was a busy man. He owned four large corporations, he had a family, and he was the president of several national boards for entrepreneurs.

At age 48, Larry found himself having recurrent instances of sickness: several common colds, one instance of pneumonia, and migraine headaches at least weekly. His work stoppages created stockpiles of work for him to do when he would return.

One of his very close friends and advisors named Donald, who was also very successful in business advised Larry. He said, "Man, you have to delegate more, but the more important thing is to spend time with God in prayer and meditation. I have been without sickness for 5 years straight since I learned how to pray. I will stop by weekly with you and we can pray together".

Donald would come over to Larry's house, turn off music that disrupted the peace, instruct the family about how to maintain an atmosphere of peace, and lead Larry into a worry-free state of rest. He would instruct him to say, "I release worries related to my work now. I release conflict and pain from my body now", and for 20 minutes, they would release anxiety and anything else that disrupts their focus from entering into the presence of God.

After about the first 20 minutes (or whenever they completed the process of release and cleansing), they would express their gratitude to God for their success, their learning lessons, and even their shortcomings. One such example was when Larry had walked out and noticed a large dent on the driver side of his Lamborghini door, he said, "I thank you Father that you protected me from hurt, harm, and danger. I thank you that despite the shortcoming of the person that hit my car, you gave them the courage to leave their insurance information and contact number. I understand that it could have been very easy and appear beneficial to leave the scene, but you instilled in them the compassion that allowed me justice."

Donald and Larry spent one hour daily cycling thru different phases of prayer. They said that about one hour into their prayer, an overwhelming presence would come upon them, and completely overwhelm their senses, so that they could not comprehend the entire experience or speak much, but became paralyzed in an ecstatic state of love and joy. At this point, their emotions could not fathom the presence, but they described it with two analogies. On some occasions, they would attempt to describe the presence as a cord being plugged into electricity with the surge of an unseen or unknown intensity that transformed them instantaneously (even in places that they were not aware needed change).

On other instances, they would describe the presence as comparable to the gold refining process; where they could feel the heat burning away unholiness and reshaping them from the inside out. Beyond the two analogies, they would just nod their heads and became speechless; unable to articulate the feeling and power of the presence. They referred to this place saying that they, "entered the Holy of Holies". Donald and Larry spent between one to three hours daily in prayer, and they noticed drastic results.

Larry was not as anxious about controlling his business. He got ideas about how to delegate some of the tasks he had been holding onto. Larry also made great connections, which enabled him to hire highly qualified staff. His body had drastically improved, with no reoccurrences of sickness. Out of gratitude, Larry donated $1 million dollars to charitable organizations that Donald owned, and their relationship grew very close. Many more blessings came causing their business affairs to prosper further, their relationships to grow, opportunities were in surplus, and the people associated with them were also blessed.

Understand how cycling thru different phases of prayer can empower you

Prayer is a liberating experience, but when we get stuck, then it is crippling. Prayer is not meant to be a time of complete asking or receiving, but rather there are phases that can enable us to get closer and more intimate in the presence of God. You do not want to dwell in one phase of prayer and ramble, but rather, cycle thru the varying phases and allow your prayer time to be a time of refreshing.

The **Relaxation Phase**

God's presence is a place of enjoyment. We cannot get the best out of our prayer time if we don't understand the place of relaxation as we come before Him. The Holy Spirit through the apostle Paul Said in Philippians 4:6: that we should "Be anxious for nothing, but in everything by prayer and supplication, with thanksgiving, let your requests be made known to God." So the first thing to do as we come into the throne room is to relax, get quiet, savor-in His presence. No anxiety, no hurry, no agitations, no trouble, but quiet rest, confidence and assurance. The Holy Spirit does not work where there is unrest, agitations and anxiety. So as you get ready to go into the place of prayer, settle in your heart that you will come into His presence relaxed.

When you attempt to pray without releasing the worries of the day, it leaves your prayer time adulterated. You focus on your phone ringing because of the possibility of important phone calls, you think about what you said that you should not have, what you did that you should not have, and so on. When you come before God, you first want to release worries, anxious thoughts, obligations, and remove distractions. Televisions, music, yelling, loud talking, or other things that take your attention away from being completely devoted to God should be removed. Just as Donald did, you want to inform those around that you are devoting time to God, so that they understand the need for solitude and do not distract you.

As a mother and a wife, at times, I have been easily distracted from my prayer time because of my son crying or my husband saying, "Honey. Can you...?". I learned to gracefully say, "I am spending some time with God. I need the television volume to stay low, the music to stay tuned to praise and worship, and save your questions for after I am finished in His presence". When I would plan my time with God, arrange meals and other events prior or afterward, and gracefully discuss my arrangements with my family, then my success rate would substantially increase.

Begin by releasing distractions that can come from your senses (being tired, hungry, thirsty, bad smells, good smells, and so on). Remove what you can: take the trash out if necessary, flush the toilet, burn incense, turn distracting music off, and so on. You want to say, "I relax my senses and focus on the holy presence of God now". Relax your body and take comfort in your prayer position, say something like, "I rest my body before God and I take rest in the mighty presence of my King". Remove electronic distractions or noises and delight in the peace of God. Control roaming thoughts by saying something like, "I take captive every thought of worry, discomfort, disadvantage. I remove every fear. I remove the access of the opposer that attempts to distract my attention from God now."

The Thanksgiving Phase

The phase of thanksgiving is where you express gratitude to God. You will find that this phase of prayer feels good. It is a great remedy for depression or dissatisfaction. When you enter into thanksgiving for what God has done for you, it changes the momentum of your thoughts, redirecting your focus from problem to solution, from what you don't have to what you do have, and it attracts greater good to come to you. Thanksgiving is where you acknowledge the grace and the faithfulness of God in your life.

It is easy to confuse the thanksgiving phase of prayer with praise, but they are different. We praise God for "who" He is but thank Him for "what" He is. When we praise God, we might not necessarily have any reason to do so, but we do because of who He is. When one reflects on creation, the wonders and marvels of God's handiwork, the sea, the sky, even the making of man, one cannot escape the idea of praising the Creator. God is wonderful. How does a fetus grow in the womb, from seed-blood, to a full grown baby with bones, eyes, nose everything-the wonders of God. So we cannot help but praise Him for it.

But when it comes to thanksgiving, you are no longer generalizing God to His entire creation; you are particularizing God to yourself; making declarations of his goodness to you. You are relating with Him because you have not only heard about Him but have seen Him in your life affairs. This is a great way to pray. The prayer of thanksgiving is a prayer that shows gratitude to God for what He has done for you as an individual.

You can say things like:

"I thank you God for the health in my body"

"I thank you for my family"

"I thank you for shelter over my head"

"I thank you for the food that I eat"

"I thank you for the connections that you have assigned me"

"I thank you for safety in my travels"

"I thank you for the clothes on my back"

"I thank you that you have sent me here with a divine purpose"

"I thank you for revelation and ideas"

It is better to get more particular. You can take the above statements and dissect them; making them more customized to your individual circumstance. Thank God for the result and the process. Sometimes, we forget to be thankful for the process that is bringing about our answers. In the book of Job, he lost his children, his property, and his health, but he understood that it was all a part of the process of greater blessing. For this reason, in Romans 8:28, Paul said, "And we know that in all things God works for the good of those who love him, who have been called according to his purpose." Know that if you can imagine it, it can be done, so express thanksgiving for the image, the process, and the result.

Jesus was always full of thanksgiving to God before and after so many of His great acts. He expressed gratitude prior to the miracle. He said by the tomb of Lazarus, "Father I thank you that you have heard me and I know you hear me always." When He fed the five thousand with five loaves and two fishes, the Scripture say, "He lifted up His eyes to Heaven and then blessed in thanksgiving and broke the bread." (Matthew 14:15-23, John 11:41-42)

The apostles also knew the power of thanksgiving, which is why in 1 Timothy 2:1-2 Paul wrote:

"I urge, then, first of all, that petitions, prayers, intercession and thanksgiving be made for all people".

Your mental picture plays a large part into your actual future. It is important to learn to be thankful to God for the pictures that we see, the picture that are created in our minds; these are proof that God has answered us.

God shows us pictures to protect and garnish our faith. To Abraham, He said, "Look up to Heaven and count the number of the stars, if you can be able to do that, so shall your descendants be." And it was said of Abraham; having seen that picture, that he believed God and it was counted for him as righteousness. Believe the picture that you see and be grateful to God for them. I believe Abraham had to live a life of gratitude afterwards, having seen those pictures.

Vision means that the creation has already taken place in the Spirit. If you see it, it means it is possible. Come in agreement with the words God spoke to Abraham, "As far as your eyes can see".

Meditate on the vision and the promises. It is important also that we not only see those pictures but ruminate on them in our minds. Think on the pictures that you see. Whether they be pictures in the mind, in vision, dreams or revelation from the word of God, think on them. For me, I believe the greatest picture one can get of God and of himself is the picture of the word of God. Get God's picture for yourself and meditate on it. His picture will last more than any other picture. Heaven and earth shall pass away, but God's word shall never pass away. (See Matthew 24:35)

The Cleansing and Releasing Phase

It is important for us to know that even the atmosphere around us is dirty and infested with sin and demons. You have met and meet with people all day long, you have said and done things that are not consistent with the word of God, so it's time to get cleaned up. It's time to confess our wrongs and ask for the cleansing blood of the Lamb of God to wash us clean from head to toe.

In the Old Testament, The Bible talks about the process of the priests before entering the Holy of Holies. They were to be clean, they wore consecrated attire, and used consecrated instruments. Prior to Jesus raising from the dead, there were animal sacrifices that were required for intentional and unintentional sins. With this, we know that after the fall, we are naturally unclean. Our thoughts and our deeds are unclean, so we must cleanse ourselves and consecrate ourselves before entering into the presence of the Most Holy King.

In the New Testament, we don't have to offer any animal or carry out a certain kind of ritual for our cleansing and purification. It says that "If we confess our sins, He is faithful and just to forgive us our sins and to cleanse us from all unrighteousness." (1 John 1:9). All we do to receive our cleansing is to admit or acknowledge our sins by way of confession, and we will have the cleansing bath of the blood of the Son of God (Jesus), by which we are purified.

The prophet Isaiah puts it this way "Come now, and let us reason together," Says the LORD, "Though your sins are like scarlet, They shall be as white as snow; Though they are red like crimson, They shall be as wool." But how will you be washed so much that you are as white as snow and wool? 1 John 1:7 answers the question saying, "But if we walk in the light as He is in the light, we have fellowship with one another, and the blood of Jesus Christ His Son cleanses us from all sin." (See Isaiah 1:18 and 1 John 1:7)

In the phase of cleansing, you are opening the fullness of yourself to God. Cleansing is very intimate because it is syncing the awareness of your sole reliance on God. In the cleansing time, you are confessing your awareness of your emptiness and need for God. You say things like:

Father, you are aware of (the specific sin that I've committed). Your word says that what I have done is wrong, and I want to be seen as upright before You. The Bible says that all have sinned and fallen short, and in this time, I have fallen. I ask for your forgiveness and the cleansing blood of Jesus to wash me inside and out, and make me clean before You."

Jesus warned us of asking for things of God when we have not freed our brothers and sisters on Earth. He said, "And whenever you stand praying, if you have anything against anyone, forgive him, that your Father in Heaven may also forgive you your trespasses." (Mark 11:25) Therefore, it is equally important in this time of cleansing to forgive as it is for you to be clean. Let go! Forgive those that have hurt and offended you. You bind yourself to stagnancy when you do not release others and harbor unforgiveness. This is the time to make a verbal statement of release. You call the person by name and say "Lord, I forgive (the person's name or description) that has hurt me and I release him, now. I let him go in the name of Jesus."

The Meditation Phase

To meditate is to think on the Word of God. This can be done either quietly in your heart or by muttering it consciously, saying it to yourself.

I remember when my spouse and I were courting. It seemed that every thought of my heart and talk of my mouth was about him. I was always thinking about him and talking about him.

The Bible is God's love letter and instruction manual for you. It tells you of how you can inherit His abundant promises, how you can overcome life obstacles, and how you can manifest your purpose on the Earth. When you read it and repeat it aloud or in thought, it increases your faith, your ability to persevere, and your success.

In this phase of prayer, begin to think on the Scriptures that are connected with your prayer. Find the promises of God in your Bible that relate to what you're praying for, and say to God, "In Your word, you promised that if I do (your deed), you will (His deed). I have abided by your word, and I am petitioning you today to release the blessings of Heaven to me as you have promised." If you have not abided by His word, but you are ready to submit to the Kingdom laws you can say, "Today, I am committing to forsake the deeds that keep me from inheriting your promise, and I am petitioning the throne of Heaven to release the blessings of Heaven to me now".

Great men and women know the power of meditation. You cannot go far in your walk with God if you do not understand the place and power of meditation. Think on the promise of God concerning that situation, muttering it to yourself and very soon you will have built a bulwark around you and your prayer, a force field that no devil can penetrate.

The Basking Phase

To bask is to derive pleasure from something or get enjoyment from something. Basking is like bathing; you are soaking in the awe of a mighty God. Don't rush out of the presence of God. Listen and allow him to speak to you. Experience the calmness of His presence. Take the time to enjoy and to savor His glory. Feel Him; let His presence and glory rub on you. Stay basking in the euphoria of His presence such that when you come out of that prayer closet, you are not only assured of answered prayer but also of His Shekinah. Just take in His presence until you are sure that you are ready to face your day with power and glory. Cycle thru the varying phases of prayer; revisiting whichever phase that you feel drawn.

The 3 Realms Of Prayer

Pastor Benny Hinn says that there are 3 phases of prayer: asking, seeking, and knocking. In Matthew 7:7, Jesus said, "Ask and it will be given to you; seek and you will find; knock and the door will be opened to you." To enter into each realm, you must allot time to be intimate with God. In the asking realm, you are in the phase of release, forgiveness, and thanksgiving. This is where you make your petitions known to God. You are aligning your words with the Word of God by saying, "God, your Word says..., therefore...". You are being open with God about your desires and how you will use them to enhance and make great the Kingdom of God.

When you are before God (in the realm of asking), it's not about you; it's about the Kingdom. You will find that access to the Kingdom is more than you could fathom thru selfishness or lust, but you must align this perspective, and ground your intentions. You should not bring uncleanliness (selfishness and lust) before God saying, "God, I want something just for me, so that I can look good, feel good, or make people think a certain way about me" (from a lustful, proud or haughty heart). How does your request advance the Kingdom? How can your blessing impact multitudes? The car, the house, the business, the job, the promotion, the money, the wife, the husband, the children, or whatever else that you may want; how can you use it to serve others? How can you commit your gifts to the service of others? God wants to bless a right heart and right mind. He can give more than you can comprehend, but you must be in harmony.

Remember in the Old Testament, when the priests were preparing themselves for entrance into the Holy of Holies, they had to cleanse themselves first. They could not enter without bringing a sacrifice and laying their sacrifice before the altar of God. After Jesus took the authority of Heaven and Earth, we do not have to give animal or blood sacrifices. Cleanse yourself with the blood of Jesus; washing yourself with the Word. The asking realm is before the altar and requires the investment of our time in intimacy with God.

The Old Testament priests could feel the aura of His presence before entering the Tent of Meeting, they could see the cloud of His presence, and they could smell the incense that was behind the curtain. In the asking realm, you are beginning to feel the aura of the presence of God, the peace, the joy, and the love. Your senses are being excited with an incomparable presence. When you have finished asking, you must be prepared to enter a new realm.

Once you have been cleansed and you have let your request be made known, then you enter the realm where you are seeking for Jesus. This is when you are basking in the awe of His holiness; the time where you are overwhelmed by the presence of such power. When you seek, you will find. When you find, and you begin to knock, God will welcome you into the Holy of Holies where your request will be agreed upon and made final. After you say, "Amen" and your prayer is complete, you must prepare for the manifestation.

Summary

- Be innovative in communication with God
- Cycle Thru Phases Of Prayer
- Prayer Phases
- Relax
- Thanksgiving
- Cleansing and releasing
- Meditation
- Basking
- Enter the 3 realms of prayer: asking, seeking, and knocking

CHAPTER EIGHT

UNDERSTAND THE DIFFERENT PRAYER TYPES

"God's desire is to not only have you experience His love, but to totally overwhelm you with His love. To have you experience it to overflowing. To have you sense, feel, taste, and touch His love for you. He really wants you to experience Him!"

— Linda Boone (Intimate Life Lessons; developing the intimacy with God you already have.)

The Story Of Dora

Dora is a God-fearing woman. She is a part of her church's intercessory ministry, and she has been active for 7 years. At her church, Dora learned to pray aloud. One year ago, Dora went on a mission trip to South America where her fellow missionaries did not pray aloud. She thought that the way that they prayed was incorrect, so she would tell them, "You are supposed to pray out of your mouth. The Bible gives several examples where people prayed out of their mouths and got results". She was so critical of the other missionaries because they prayed silently, and eventually, Dora was sent home before the mission was completed.

Sometimes Pray Aloud and Sometimes Pray In Your Heart

There is a place for praying aloud and there is a place for praying quietly in your mind and heart. It is not the amount of shouting that gets the job done, but the relationship with Jesus that gets your prayers answered. Volume should be made suitable for your environment because the Bible warns against prayer that is done for the sake of attention or disorderly worship, but it also invites us to pour our petitions before God. We know that a balance must be made between being intimate with God and respectful of those in your environment. Similar to Dora's situation, there are people who have been taught silent prayer only, and prayer aloud may be a surprise to them. On the contrary, there are people like Dora who have only been exposed to prayer aloud. Both quiet prayer and prayer aloud should be in your arsenal. Your body was made to be able to communicate with and without volume, and both expressions should be balanced to grow your relationship with God, while also maintaining the humility and respect to allow others to grow in their relationships with God around you. Prayer should not be done to distract others from being able to enter the presence of God themselves. In corporate settings, you must discern whether your prayers aloud will distract others. In your alone time, you can pour your petitions before God in whichever way you would like.

I think the story of Hannah has a lot to say about this. 1 Samuel 1:9-19 says:

"So Hannah arose after they had finished eating and drinking in Shiloh. Now Eli the priest was sitting on the seat by the doorpost of the tabernacle of the LORD. And she *was* in bitterness of soul, and prayed to the LORD and wept in anguish. Then she made a vow and said, "O LORD of hosts, if You will indeed look on the affliction of Your maidservant and remember me, and not forget Your maidservant, but will give Your maidservant a male child, then I will give him to the LORD all the days of his life, and no razor shall come upon his head." And it happened, as she continued praying before the LORD, that Eli watched her mouth. Now Hannah spoke in her heart; only her lips moved, but her voice was not heard. Therefore Eli thought she was drunk. So Eli said to her, "How long will you be drunk? Put your wine away from you!" And Hannah answered and said, "No, my lord, I *am* a woman of sorrowful spirit. I have drunk neither wine nor intoxicating drink, but have poured out my soul before the LORD. "Do not consider your maidservant a wicked woman, for out of the abundance of my complaint and grief I have spoken until now." Then Eli answered and said, "Go in peace, and the God of Israel grant your petition which you have asked of Him." And she said, "Let your maidservant find favor in your sight." So the woman went her way and ate, and her face was no longer *sad*.

Now Hannah spoke in her heart; only her lips moved but her voice was not heard. She knew the secret of praying in her heart and Samuel is the proof that God heard her. We should learn that art from Hannah. She practiced the intimate movement of pouring her heart to God in a discrete way that allowed no one, but God to understand what she was saying.

In other instances, shouting to God or prayers aloud are useful. In Psalms 47:1, David said "Clap your hands, all you nations; shout to God with cries of joy." Prayers aloud in a setting where you are not disruptive and your intention is pure, or prayers in a private place are settings where prayers aloud can be perfect for communication with the Most High King.

Prayers For Healing

Healing is a byproduct of prayer and intimacy with God. In her book, *The Dynamic Laws For Healing*, Catherine Ponders says, "Health and salvation are the same...Permanent health comes from freeing the mind of its beliefs in ignorance and sin, rather than adding to that belief". On another occasion she said, "Although man is only about 2 percent physical and 98 percent mental and spiritual, the average person spends about 98 percent of his time thinking about the 2 percent of his physical nature!" She says that you cannot try to attain health from outward in, but rather, from inward out. This is the difference between a "cure" and "healing". Curing focuses on eliminating immediate distress and can be solved simply by seeking medical help, but healing, on the other hand, is focused on permanence and wholeness. Healing frees, delivers, completes, and reforms from the inside out, therefore, no repeat treatment is necessary because the spirit, soul, and body have become whole.

Typically, when sickness is materialized in the body, you must act. You must visualize wholeness, forgive, learn the true power of salvation and God's grace, and ward off the kingdom of darkness. In the presence of God, the healing balm naturally will flow into those wounds of yours bringing grace, healing, and deliverance.

In his studies scientist and relationship expert, Dr. John Gottman was able to show the effect of language on the body. He proved that words of criticism, contempt, defensiveness, and internalizing poisonous words thru stonewalling are all harmful to the body.

Critical speech are words that destroy dreams. They include

fallacies and laws. They suggest error, fault, lack, or dysfunction by suggesting false trends such as, "always" and "never" to give a larger illusion of failure. When you say, "you always!", or "you never!" , it usually does not have truth, but instead, it makes the illusion of defeat seem more likely.

Words or behavior of contempt is when a person is undervalued. You are a child of God and you should be treated that way. Whether in customer service or in a family setting, contemptuous behavior can be poisonous when given or received. Contempt can be blanketed in sarcasm, prejudice, segregation, and stereotypes.

Defensiveness is when you try to defend your character with words. Wisdom tells us that defense of character is not necessary, but when criticism or contempt enter conversation, defensiveness is the typical response. In Proverbs 27:19, King Solomon says, "As water reflects the face, so one's life reflects the heart." You do not have to defend your character because it is reflected in your life.

When many poisonous words (words of failure, low esteem, fault, lack, and dysfunction) and poisonous actions (physical or sexual abuse, body language suggesting rejection, or poor habits accumulated to distract from trauma), it is not healthy, and greatly affects the health. Some of the effect of poisonous words are a weakened immune system, sickness, disease, cardiovascular trauma (high blood pressure, elevated temperature, increased heart rate), and many more. For the sake of your health, it is pertinent for you to transform your speech if you speak using poisonous words, transform your actions, treat people in agreement with God's view of them, and it is equally important for you to avoid surrounding yourself with people that speak or act negatively towards you. For this reason, in Romans 8:1-2, Apostle Paul warned against this type of behavior by saying, "Therefore, there is now no condemnation for those who are in Christ Jesus, because through Christ Jesus the law of the Spirit who gives life has set you free from the law of sin and death."

Healing cannot flow into a heart callused with unforgiveness, so you must learn to let go for your sake. Forgiveness is a pertinent practice to restore the body. In unforgiveness, parts of the soul are scattered amongst to every person that you believe that you are holding hostage or ensuring justice. You must pick up those scattered pieces by freeing yourself from your negative attachment to the people (feeling of injustice or betrayal) that you have yet to forgive.

You must think back and identify the source of the sickness or disease. God does not genetically design humans to fail, but there can be choices that affect generations.

The Story Of Zoey and her family

Zoey was born into an African American family that struggled with obesity. She loved ballet, but she felt like an outcast being overweight in a leotard. Zoey wanted to transform, but for more than four generations, she was able to trace back obesity, high blood pressure, and diabetes. Her mother taught her how to cook, her mother's mother taught her how to cook, and so on.

Zoey realized that her family's taste buds had grown accustom to receiving sensation from unhealthy foods. When Zoey did research to discover the root of their unhealthy cooking behavior, she discovered that their cooking originated in slavery. The slaves would receive the leftover parts of the meat such as the intestines, the feet, noses, and sources of meat that slaveowners did not eat.

The slaves turned the leftovers into their own cuisine, and passed down the traditions generationally. Zoey's family still sought out the portions of the meat that were "leftovers" of the slaveowners.

Zoey decided that she would have to dump everything that she learned about food and nutrition. She decided to apply the biblical Levitical diet to her life. She applied Leviticus 3:16-17 which said:

"All the fat is the LORD's. "'This is a lasting ordinance for the generations to come, wherever you live:You must not eat any fat or any blood.'"

Then she went further to apply Leviticus 11:1-3 which says:

"The LORD said to Moses and Aaron, "Say to the Israelites: 'Of all the animals that live on land, these are the ones you may eat: You may eat any animal that has a divided hoof and that chews the cud."

She would cut the fat from her food, cook them until no blood was seen, and she was selective about the meat that she ate. She focused her attention on beef, chicken, and fish with scales. She began reading about healthy eating, she made meal plans, tracked her caloric intake, and implemented an exercise regimen. Within three months, Zoey had lost 35 pounds and felt closer to her dream of being a ballerina.

The Root Of Your Disadvantage Does Not Come From God, So Identify The Root, and Pull it up!

Zoey had identified the root of her family's genetic disorders, but first she had to understand that God does not design people disadvantaged. Mankind has so much power that we are able to modify animal and human genetics with chemicals! We put so many varying chemicals into food, and the majority of the world pays no attention to the poisons that crawl down their throats, therefore, their families are affected in multiples of ways. Babies are born with more than one gender or handicap, people are blind, some cannot hear, some have cardiovascular disturbances, and so on. The good news is that we have a forgiving God who takes away the consequences of our sin and makes us whole when we earnestly repent.

Metaphysician, Charles Fillmore said that germs are a result of thought. They are a result of anger, revenge, jealousy, fear, impure thinking, and many other mind activities. He said that germs are intelligent and respond when they are called. In his words, "A change of mind will change the character of germs".

Our thoughts, actions, and words make alliances with the Kingdom of God or the kingdom of darkness. By way of our actions and words, we reap consequences of blessing or curse. Sickness and disease is a consequence and demands salvation that comes thru prayer and a relationship with God.

Forgiveness is one aspect of healing. It begins by identifying the root cause. Did someone do something to you? Did you do something to someone else? Is this a punishment that is being passed down generationally? Is this punishment by association? When the root of the illness is unforgiveness, you must identify the unforgiveness that is connected to the illness in your body. Where is the transgression? Who broke Kingdom laws? Failing to forgive another person is a breach of Kingdom laws and does reap consequences (whether reactive or not). Take self-responsibility for your role in the situation and relinquish control of the justice. God will handle it. You can ask God to show you the root by saying, "Father of all. My body is manifesting illness that I believe may be attached to unforgiveness. I ask that you would show me the root of this?"

If healing has not yet manifested because God is teaching you of His grace, the scenario works a bit different. In 2 Corinthians 12, Paul had a thorn in his side that pained him so much, and redirected his attention to God. At times, your sickness can be your incentive for drawing close to God. In this time, God will show you that His grace can sustain you. For many of us, when we receive from God, we turn our backs. When God teaches you His grace, He keeps you returning for His peace. He relieves your pain, but He reminds you of your wholeness thru Him and emptiness without Him. You can show submissiveness to the lesson thru gratitude. You can thank God for redirecting your attention to His perfect peace, the deliverance that he can offer, and the salvation that came threw His son.

Your story is not for you. Your story fills a bigger picture; it draws people to the Kingdom of God. People can either learn from your blessing or your consequence, they learn from your healing and your grace, or they learn from your trial and your victory.

To receive healing thru prayer, you must be firm in faith. With healing and dysfunction in the body as a distraction, it can be very difficult to stand firm in visualizing your wholeness. Receiving healing as a byproduct of prayer means that until your healing is made manifest, you must be persistent in renewing your mind with the vision of your healed body. Increase your Bible intake and read the manufacturing manual (the Bible) that tells you how the body was designed to operate. You will also find that the Bible discloses stories where sickness and disease were healed, and reading them will increase your faith. The body was designed good, therefore, healing is a natural law.

Prayers For Protection

Even with locks, doors, windows, cameras, bars, and buildings, breaking and entering still takes place. Despite the earthly law, the government, and their consequences, justice thru man is not a 100% guaranty. As you go out, you witness injustice, you may not always advocate for what's right, and you are held accountable for your actions. We breach moral and spiritual territories all of the time! The only way that we can assure our safety from harm and our freedom from imputed punishment is to stay submitted to God and pray for protection. In prayers for protection, you invite Heaven to protect you.

In prayers for protection you invite the Heavenly hosts and you deny evil access (spoken of in later chapters). You create spiritual structures with your words, and block the entrance of spiritual opponents.

Prayers Of Illumination

Illumination is a condition of spiritual awareness; an enlightenment of the spirit. Paul had an understanding of prayers of illumination; hence his prayer for the Ephesian Church recorded in Ephesians 1:15-23. It says:

"Therefore I also, after I heard of your faith in the Lord Jesus and your love for all the saints, do not cease to give thanks for you, making mention of you in my prayers: that the God of our Lord Jesus Christ, the Father of glory, may give to you the spirit of wisdom and revelation in the knowledge of Him, the eyes of your understanding being enlightened; that you may know what is the hope of His calling, what are the riches of the glory of His inheritance in the saints, and what is the exceeding greatness of His power toward us who believe, according to the working of His mighty power which He worked in Christ when He raised Him from the dead and seated Him at His right hand in the Heavenly places, far above all principality and power and might and dominion, and every name that is named, not only in this age but also in that which is to come. And He put all things under His feet, and gave Him to be head over all things to the church, which is His body, the fullness of Him who fills all in all."

Paul prayed for the spirit of wisdom and revelation for the Ephesian church, and added the eyes of their understanding may be enlightened or illuminated; resulting in their increased knowledge. This type of prayer is what opens us up for fresh ideas, the revelation of the word, the exact knowledge that we need to enter into our place in Christ. Evil ideas are running rampant on the Earth. Our world needs to be refueled by the Heavenly ideas of those that submit themselves to the will of God.

Prayers Of Union

In John 17, Jesus prayed a prayer of union. He said:

"I do not pray for these alone, but also for those who will believe in Me through their word; "that they all may be one, as You,

Father, are in Me, and I in You; that they also may be one in Us, that the world may believe that You sent Me. "And the glory which You gave Me I have given them, that they may be one just as We are one: "I in them, and You in Me; that they may be made perfect in one, and that the world may know that You have sent Me, and have loved them as You have loved Me. "Father, I desire that they also whom You gave Me may be with Me where I am, that they may behold My glory which You have given Me; for You loved Me before the foundation of the world. "O righteous Father! The world has not known You, but I have known You; and these have known that You sent Me. "And I have declared to them Your name, and will declare it, that the love with which You loved Me may be in them, and I in them.""

Satan dreads unity! We are so powerful when we join together! It is this place of oneness that he does not want the family and the church to come to. For he knows that when the husband and the wife are one, when the church is one, even a single congregation is one, his arsenal will be destroyed completely and his kingdom will collapse. But I sure know that God does answer Jesus when He prays and this prayer must be answered in your life, family, and ministry.

Prayers Of Tongues

Tongues are a spiritual gift that were used in the Bible. At times, tongues were interpreted by other people, and understood to be an inspired native language other than that of the speaker. Paul calls it mystery prayers. He said he who speaks in an inspired tongue, speaks mysteries to God in the spirit and not to men. The Bible tells us that tongues can be a language of Heaven or Earth; one spoken by other men or by angels. Tongues only edify the speaker unless they can be interpreted. When one speaks or prays in tongues, his spirit (the real person) prays. The power of prayer in tongues is that it is void of thought, but rather, it is direct spiritual communication from man to God. Similar to electronic devices syncing up to download information from another device, speaking in tongues allows the speaker to be reprogrammed to the consciousness of God.

The gift of tongues has been misused on many occasions and inequality has resulted from its misuse. Some people babble in tongues in corporate settings without interpreting, others think that people who speak in tongues are better or worse than those who don't, others think that tongues identify those who are going to Heaven, and still yet others ban the use of tongues. The use of tongues are biblical, but with order. The Bible does not support those who say that they signify the assurance of salvation.

Using tongues in prayer to God can add greater intimacy for those that possess the gift. The prayer language is not one that is understood by the kingdom of darkness, therefore, there is no interruption or twisting causing misunderstanding. Instead, the tongues are strictly for spiritual renewal. Isaiah 28:11 explains tongues by saying, "For with stammering lips and another tongue He will speak to this people."

Pray While Fasting

Another type of prayer is fasting prayer. Fasting is denying yourself of something to make a statement of commitment to God. We cannot undermine or underestimate the place of fasting in the cycle of prayer. Jesus demanded that we fast, not for religious purposes but for grace and power. The Bible has record of men and women like Moses or Jesus who fasted 40 days and 40 nights, and changed the course of their lives, destinies and nations.

Fasting is an increased symbol of faith and commitment in lieu of prayer. It is a way of saying to God, "I am denying myself the needs of my physical body because I know that I need more than physical sustenance to live this life. I need You to fill my cup." It is a symbol of understanding that you live on more than bread and water alone. It shows God that you understand that spiritual power is more sustaining than anything that you can achieve on the Earth. Fasting increases your self-control, it assists in the process of cleansing, and it removes unclean things that you may have put into your body that are now streaming thru your blood. There are some mountains that will not come down; there are some situations that will not break until you add fasting to your prayers. Fasting is going the extra mile.

Summary

- Understand the purpose and use of different prayer types
- Be appropriate for your environment by sometimes praying in your heart, and sometimes in your mind
- Thanksgiving
- Illumination
- Healing
- Protection
- Union
- Tongues
- Fasting

CHAPTER NINE

PRAY THROUGH YOUR ART

"Art is communication."

— Madeleine L'Engle, *Walking on Water: Reflections on Faith and Art*

The Story Of Alyssa

Alyssa was born without vocal capabilities. She was able to write and used her writing as a form of expression, but beyond that, she had an immense ability to paint and dance. At times, she would write letters, but on other occasions, she would develop massive dance productions that could move people to laughter or tears within seconds.

When her mother passed away, her siblings asked her to write a poem for their mother's funeral. In response to the request, she wrote her siblings and said, "I apologize, but words will not be able to express mom's meaning or impact on me, so I will be choreographing a dance and painting a background that will better illustrate her life impact and tell God, "Thank you" for her life.

At the funeral, as soon as the curtain opened and the background set was seen, you could hear the sniffling from amongst the audience. The lighting was dim and the chosen dance genre was modern. Alyssa danced across the stage without music. She carried a ribbon that symbolized the companionship and building that her mother did in the lives of all those that were around her. The background set illustrated the growth of a fetus into an adult, and Allysa danced from one side of the stage to the other with the ribbon illustrating how her mother taught her from dependence to interdependence the interconnectedness of us all, and the beauty of life thru good times and bad.

Your Talent is a Communication Portal

Through your talent, you can pour your petitions before God. Alyssa was able to illustrate her message better thru dance and visual art than she could thru spoken or written words. Like Alyssa, God has bestowed you with talents that can be used to communicate in ways that words cannot. Melodies that you can sing in song, pictures that you can capture in imagery, or dances that you can use as expressions to God can communicate thoughts and messages that words may not be able to articulate.

Sing Prayers

By the intonation of your voice, and the rhythm you assign, you can express the desperate needs of your heart. You can express how you feel; whether you are in sorrow or laughter, joy or pain. When words have abandoned your mind, you can muster a hum or a song that communicates to God what you are pondering in your heart. 1 Corinthians 14:15, Paul said that he will pray with the spirit and would also pray with the understanding, that he would sing with the spirit, and that he would also sing with the understanding.

David wrote many of the Psalms as songs to God. He illustrated many emotions and feelings in his songs to God. You can also sing songs that have already been written, but are consistent with the message that you want to communicate, you can listen for the songs of the angels and sing alongside them, or you can spontaneously sing songs of prayer to God.

Visual art as prayer

Visual art: painting, sculpting, glassmaking, photography communicated messages to God and man. You can record your revelations thru visual art, but you can also use your visual art to communicate to God. You can depict an image of something that you want to manifest.

I painted a picture of my son with the hand of Jesus on his head. Anytime I see this picture, I come in agreement with the idea that I want the hand of God to touch my generations.

You can also make visual statements of declaration, love, thanksgiving, or anything else thru visual art. You see artists that have painted what has been revealed to them. As a result of visual artists, the throne of God, the angels, and other Heavenly things have been attached to a picture in our minds. Use your art to encourage and communicate to the Kingdom of God.

Dancing as prayer

When you watch the Jewish priests offering and burning incense to the Lord, you would see a lot of moves and gesticulation, and all is done in prayer and the worship of the Lord.

Dance is healthy as it exercises our bodies, but also it expresses things thru our movement and posture. For example, we know that when a baby has tilted his head back and raised his hands upwards, it is likely he wants to be carried, the same motions reveal to God our level of surrender. We can walk lowly or dignified, and communicate to God and others around our level of desperation or dignity. Dance can be used to increase our joy and communicate to God simultaneously. We can choreograph movements that collectively tell Him how grateful we are for the works that He has done in our lives. Dance added onto other prayer phases and types can definitely add greater enjoyment in your prayer time.

Praise as you pray

In praise, we speak, sing, and dance to express how magnificent God is. His creation is beyond the ingenuity of man, so we invest time as we are cycling thru the varying prayer phases and types to sing to Him and tell Him of how awesome of an engineer He is. Who can combine one hydrogen molecule with two oxygens? No one, but God, so for reasons as these, we praise Him during our prayer time.

Summary

- Pray thru your art - Thru your talent, you can pour your petitions before God

- You can use singing to pray

- You can use visual art to pray

- You can use dancing to pray

- You can praise as you pray

CHAPTER TEN

ALLY WITH THE HEAVENLY HOSTS

"The great comfort in knowing that angels minister to believers
in Christ is that God Himself sends them to us."

— Billy Graham (The Heaven Answer Book)

Victor and Gabriela were a loving couple. They met in Brazil on a business trip for their internet marketing companies. Victor is a citizen of the US and Gabriela was a citizen of Ethiopia. Their business trip lasted four months (most of which they knew they would be married). They had the chance to build a strong connection. Every night, after their business meetings were over, they would meet at precisely 7 o'clock to talk, do Bible study, and learn new things about one another. When they separated, they knew that it would be difficult to maintain their relationship because of the difference in their time zones, their work schedules, and the possible negative input from others (being that they did not have common connections). Even with the obstacles, Victor gave Gabriela a promise ring and vowed to marry her.

After ten months of separation, a lot of difficulty with the immigration process, and high international calling expenses, Gabriela began to question herself asking, "Is this relationship really the one that God has for me?" She began to forget about the spiritual connection that she had with Victor when they were together. Everyone was advising her to leave him alone and find someone from her country. They would say, "You don't have to experience a mystery relationship. Instead, you can marry someone where you know the integrity of his family and that they will treat you well". Gabriela told Victor, "I want to take a break from talking with you about marriage. I think that the immigration problems may be a sign that we are not in God's timing. Maybe, I was riding on my emotions instead of submitting to the voice of God. I want a sign from God."

Victor decided to pray. He said, "Father, I thank you for allowing me to feel love and to connect with a woman in a way that makes me desire marriage. I love Gabriela with every fiber of my being. I believe that together in marriage, we can accomplish the purpose that you have assigned us both here to accomplish. I ask that you would cleanse both of us of any infirmities and allow us to stand upright before you. I remove assignments from the enemy to hinder the divine movement of love in our lives. I speak to her angel now and I say, 'You know the Kingdom of Heaven is the place of love, and you know that Gabriela and I manifest a Kingdom love. I ask you now to speak words to remind Gabriela of our Heavenly love. Gabriel, angel in authority of message distribution in Heaven, I ask you now to send angels to confirm the presence of Heavenly love between Gabriella and I now. Thank you Father that your word has authorized everything that I have asked. I walk away knowing that it is done in Jesus's name. Amen."

That day, Gabriela went mountain climbing with two of her friends. As she was climbing, her harness snapped and she started to descend at hefty speeds. As she was falling helplessly, her friends screamed, "Gabriela!", but no one could help her. Suddenly, something that glowed tipped her onto an avalanche; preventing her from further descent. She sat on the avalanche crying and breathing unbearably. Then a voice said, "Gabriela. Don't be afraid. I was sent to catch you and bring a message to you. Your Father has heard your prayer requesting confirmation regarding your relationship with Victor. I am here to confirm to you that the love that you have for one another has been granted by the Kingdom of God."

Be aware of the spiritual things

There is so much that cannot be seen by the eye in the world that we live in. God spoke thru a prophet in Jeremiah 29:11 saying, "For I know the plans I have for you," declares the LORD, "plans to prosper you and not to harm you, plans to give you hope and a future." This passage tells us that God desires for us to have a prosperous future; it does not describe pain and suffering nor does it describe an end. Bad things happen in effort to impose eternal damnation on you. There is a Kingdom of Light and a kingdom of darkness; one intends life and good, and the other intends death and bad. God's plans are always good, but there are alternate forces that fight to prevent His goodness from reaching you. There is a physical world that we live in, and a spiritual world that governs it. You and I have to be conscious of the fact that our world has a higher population of spiritual beings than physical beings, and the spiritual governs the physical; never vice versa.

God is spirit, who made the physical world. In order to relate with God, we must believe and accept therefore the reality of the world that cannot be seen with the optical eyes. The creations of God are proof that He is real even if we cannot see Him. Satan is spirit and his demons are too, we cannot see them, but we can tell of their presence by the manifestations of evil in our world.

Your prayer life and intimacy with God grows your relationship, strength, and ability to fight off evil spirits. You must develop this prayer practice in order to become a force to reckon with in regards to your success on this Earth.

Develop a consciousness of the spiritual. The realm of the spirit is all around us. It is the basic ingredient for everything that we see. By the spirit, the one creature that omits a thing and the other that demands it are both supplied; thus is the basis for God's creation of the ecosystem. The spirit cannot be escaped or ignored; it is a presence whether you decide to confront it or not, whether you choose to be informed about it or not.

Develop a relationship with the angels

Alliance with the angels is a part of our inheritance thru Jesus Christ. Because of his blood, we have access to the army of Heaven. The physical realm is only a response to the spiritual realm. In learning the realm of the spirit, one pertinent task is to understand our allies. God and His angels are allies while Satan and his demons are opponents; these are the key components of the spiritual realm. The physical realm responds to the alliances that we make with each one of our choices.

For choices that are submissive to the words of God, the physical realm responds by blessing inhabitants of the world. For choices that are submissive to the kingdom of darkness, the physical realm responds by cursing the inhabitants of the world. We reap blessings or curses, happiness or sadness, enjoyment or pain as a response to our choices that are for or against the will of God.

If things are not going right, you know that the kingdom of darkness has been invited into your midst by your choices, the choices of your forefathers, or someone in your midst. When the first commandment (which directs you to love God first and make all other people and things a latter priority) is broken, the Bible describes the consequence by saying:

"You shall not bow down to them or worship them; for I, the Lord your God, am a jealous God, punishing the children for the sin of the parents to the third and fourth generation of those who hate me,".

When you have identified the kingdom of darkness in your presence, you ward them off thru authoritative prayer, the communication with the allies of God, and the use of the armor of God. The Bible gives a lot of insight about the angels and how we can coordinate with them. Hebrews 1 describes the role of the angels as allies in ministry in the hierarchy of God. It describes that Jesus holds the authority of Heaven, and that the angels are submitted to him. Therefore, when man is petitioning the Kingdom of God for things that are congruent with the goals of Heaven, we can request for alliance with the angels.

Invite The Angels In Your Midst

In Psalms, King David invited the angels to praise alongside him and to go to war on his behalf. King David also forecasted for us how the angels will work with us to advance the Kingdom of God, to praise alongside us, protect us, stand guard, and perform miracles alongside us. Regarding the hierarchy, in Psalms 8:4-6 he said, "what is mankind that you are mindful of them, human beings that you care for them? You have made them a little lower than the angels and crowned them with glory and honor. You made them rulers over the works of your hands; you put everything under their feet:" Regarding their ability to protect and stand guard, King David said, "The angel of the Lord encamps around those who fear him, and he delivers them."

In Genesis, we see the angels delivering prophetic messages, commuting from Heaven to Earth in Jacob's dream, and inflicting the judgement of God on the people of Sodom and Gomorrah. At times, the angels were visible to the optical eye and expressed human desires (as was the case when Abraham was visited or when the angels interbred with the beautiful women).

The Bible tells us that the angels have the ability to make godly or ungodly choices. Like man, the angels are also subject to consequences, but the only consequences spoken of in the Bible was being thrown from Heaven to Earth and eternal damnation. In Revelations, Michael and the warring angels of God removed Satan and the angels that followed him from Heaven, and hurled them to the Earth.

In Matthew, the angels were appointed by God to send prophetic messages, they tended to Jesus after he was tempted by Satan, they collaborated with Jesus, and he spoke of their participation in gaining us eternal glory. In Acts, the angels participated in the deliverance of the first century ministers from the hands of the Roman government and by sending the message of the resurrection of Jesus to the gentiles.

In the Bible, people like Abraham, Moses, and Jesus used their alliance with the angels to successfully carry out pertinent purposeful tasks. When Abraham sent his servant to find a wife for Isaac, he said, "The Lord, before whom I have walked faithfully, will send his angel with you and make your journey a success, so that you can get a wife for my son from my own clan and from my father's family."

When God was leading the people of Israel to their promise land, He introduced angelic forces saying, "See, I am sending an angel ahead of you to guard you along the way and to bring you to the place I have prepared. Pay attention to him and listen to what he says. Do not rebel against him; he will not forgive your rebellion, since my Name is in him."

When Daniel was thrown into the Lion's den for mere share of jealousy, it was an angel of the Lord that delivered him. Daniel said: "The Lord has sent His angels to shut the Lions' mouth." Praise God for the ministry of angels!

In Matthew, Jesus tells us that the angels are a part of God's eternal plan, we will eventually be like them in that we will not marry in Heaven, they will return with him, and participate in the judgement of the world. Regarding the angels' participation in the last days, he said, "And he will send his angels with a loud trumpet call, and they will gather his elect from the four winds, from one end of the Heavens to the other."

The angels have been described as being larger and more powerful than humans. In Matthew, the movement of one angel caused an earthquake! Matthew 28:2 says, "There was a violent earthquake, for an angel of the Lord came down from Heaven and, going to the tomb, rolled back the stone and sat on it."

Regarding our invisible allies, Ron Phillips, pastor of the internationally televised Abba's House Church, attests to the birth of his relationship with the angels. He describes several instances of interaction with our Heavenly allies. On one occasion, he said that an angel saved him in a near-death loss of vehicle control. He describes how his car was sliding on ice, doing 360 degree turns alongside a 800-900 foot avalanche. He saw a glow (an angel) maneuver the vehicle, then a glowing figure rode alongside him until he drove home in safety. At this point, after years of developing his relationships with the angels, he talks about their presence within his church. Joy angels are seated in some areas of his sanctuary and make people that sit amongst them burst into uncontrollable laughter, in other areas of his sanctuary, there are angels with other assignments; all of them benefit the congregation and bring sanctity to their ministry.

The Scripture teaches us that every individual born into this world has an angel that is assigned by God to him or her to walk and to monitor the affairs of his or her life. You have an angel and I have one too. An account of Jesus amongst young children in the book of Matthew says:

"At that time the disciples came to Jesus, saying, "Who then is greatest in the kingdom of Heaven?" Then Jesus called a little child to Him, set him in the midst of them, and said, "Assuredly, I say to you, unless you are converted and become as little children, you will by no means enter the kingdom of Heaven."Therefore whoever humbles himself as this little child is the greatest in the kingdom of Heaven. "Take heed that you do not despise one of these little ones, for I say to you that in Heaven their angels always see the face of My Father who is in Heaven. (Matthew 18:1-4, 10)

We don't lose our angels when we grow. God does not take our angels from us when we grow up. They are always with us, but we must know, and exercise the privilege that can come along with our alliance.

Understand angelic roles

The Heavenly hierarchy includes the seraphim, cherubim, archangels, and those that walk among us. Each has a different appearance which is described in the Bible.

The Seraphim are described in Isaiah 6:1-6. The scripture says:

In the year that King Uzziah died, I saw the Lord, high and exalted, seated on a throne; and the train of his robe filled the temple. Above him were seraphim, each with six wings: With two wings they covered their faces, with two they covered their feet, and with two they were flying. And they were calling to one another:

"Holy, holy, holy is the Lord Almighty;

the whole earth is full of his glory."

At the sound of their voices the doorposts and thresholds shook and the temple was filled with smoke.

"Woe to me!" I cried. "I am ruined! For I am a man of unclean lips, and I live among a people of unclean lips, and my eyes have seen the King, the Lord Almighty."

Then one of the seraphim flew to me with a live coal in his hand, which he had taken with tongs from the altar. With it he touched my mouth and said, "See, this has touched your lips; your guilt is taken away and your sin atoned for."

From the passage, we know that the seraphim were posted above the throne of God with six wings. The power of their voices caused the atmosphere to shake!

The Cherubim

In addition to the seraphim, the Bible recurrently speaks about the cherubim. The cherubim have been known to guard the holy and sacred things near the presence of God. In the Old Testament, God instructed the Israelites to place an image of the cherubim on the ark of the covenant. In between the wings of the cherubim was the place where the presence of God was known to be. Not many passages clearly describe their appearance, but in Ezekial 10:9-14, Ezekial describes his vision of the Lord. He said:

(Under the wings of the cherubim could be seen what looked like human hands.) I looked, and I saw beside the cherubim four wheels, one beside each of the cherubim; the wheels sparkled like topaz. As for their appearance, the four of them looked alike; each was like a wheel intersecting a wheel. As they moved, they would go in any one of the four directions the cherubim faced; the wheels did not turn about as the cherubim went. The cherubim went in whatever direction the head faced, without turning as they went. Their entire bodies, including their backs, their hands and their wings, were completely full of eyes, as were their four wheels. I heard the wheels being called "the whirling wheels." Each of the cherubim had four faces: One face was that of a cherub, the second the face of a human being, the third the face of a lion, and the fourth the face of an eagle."

Regarding the atmospheric shift in the presence of the cherubim, Ezekial said, "The sound of the wings of the cherubim could be heard as far away as the outer court, like the voice of God Almighty when he speaks." This passage tells us that their wings were loud enough to be heard outside of the dense, stone temple built by King Solomon.

The Archangels

The Bible particularly mentioned two archangels by name who are the helm of affairs of the kingdom of God. They are angel Michael and angel Gabriel.

The angel, Michael, is a warring angel; one who leads defense operations for the Kingdom of God. The Bible describes several wartime spiritual operations that took place under Michael's leadership.

Psalms 91:10-12 tells us how the angels can defend you. It says, "no harm will overtake you, no disaster will come near your tent. For he will command his angels concerning you to guard you in all your ways; they will lift you up in their hands, so that you will not strike your foot against a stone." Similar to the rescue noted in the story of Victor and Gabriela, God can also send His angels to stop you from split second incidents that can threaten your life.

Gabriel leads in carrying Heavenly correspondence between Heaven and Earth. Many of the messages sent to Earth from Heaven are messages of warning or assurance. Gabriel has successfully lead angels in distributing messages across physical and spiritual realms with such sanctity that mankind has always been awed when visited.

Angels Walking Among Us

In Genesis, the Bible tells of two occasions where Abraham came in contact with angels that appeared in human form. On one instance, three angels were passing by the area where Abraham had settled. He went and pleaded that they should not pass him by without eating and taking some things with them to continue their journey, and they agreed. Genesis 18:7-10 says:

Then he ran to the herd and selected a choice, tender calf and gave it to a servant, who hurried to prepare it. He then brought some curds and milk and the calf that had been prepared, and set these before them. While they ate, he stood near them under a tree.

"Where is your wife Sarah?" they asked him.

"There, in the tent," he said.

Then one of them said, "I will surely return to you about this time next year,and Sarah your wife will have a son."

Without prior introduction, the angels asked him about his wife, Sarah, and they provided prophesy to them. On the other occasion that Abraham came in contact with angels in human form, they came to take out justice on the land of Sodom and Gomorrah. With these two passages, we know that they can partake of human deeds, they can wear human flesh, they can walk amongst us, they have access to information that pertains to the future, and we can interact with them as we can with other humans. The Bible tells us that the phenomena of angels walking amongst us still exist. Paul said, "Do not forget to show hospitality to strangers, for by so doing some people have shown hospitality to angels without knowing it."

Angels are God's messengers of deliverance, healing and help. When you pray, God uses angels to love and protect what you love, face a common enemy with you, share your allegiances and loyalties, and operate for you in the enemy's territory . They can send comfort in places that you can not physically extend to, they can send messages to every realm and territory, they fight a fierce fight in the joint authority of God and man, they can see both physical and spiritual realms and protect you with precision, and the Bible does not describe any limitation in regards to the speed of their response or physical limitations. You send a prayer and angels immediately respond, they are not limited by speed, time, or any other natural laws. Angels are spiritual beings that can defy physical algorithms. They are a mighty force and your utmost allies. They are God's messengers in bringing you answers to prayers.

Study their history

In the present and throughout history, God intervened on many occasions thru angels. We can see them bringing God's judgment upon a person, a group of people, a city or a nation. We can see them bringing God's deliverance to individuals, people and nations. Because of their supernatural strength, 1 Kings 19:35 shows that following the command of God and when under the authority of God, one angel destroyed a whole army of over a hundred thousand in one night! It says, "That night the angel of the Lord went out and put to death a hundred and eighty-five thousand in the Assyrian camp. When the people got up the next morning—there were all the dead bodies!" Let me remind you that the Assyrian army was the world-power at this time, and according to their historic records, they were at their peak power!

The strength of the angels far outweighs human physical ability. Angels are not bound by gravity, and a lot of our human technology has been designed to give us a fraction of their innate abilities. Mankind has designed many highly demanded industries that can only give a small fraction of the angels' abilities: transportation, communication, and music are mere imitations of something that has been innovated thousands of times more superior in Heaven. Many describe their wings and their flight abilities. If you have concerns that you feel limited from defending because of your own physical abilities, invite angelic allies to defend your case. Angels accomplish supernatural tasks; things that we cannot make machines strong enough to complete!

Invite their partnership in your ministry

We all need angels; you need them and I need them. It is very important to develop your friendship with the angels as partners. They have understanding beyond language barriers. The Bible was written in both Hebrew and Greek. We know that many people spoke many different languages throughout the Bible and the angels were still able to ally with them. Open your mouth, believe God to give you words that are understood across spiritual realms, and invite them in your midst. When you speak to God, ask Him to keep His angels surrounding you, making your statements understood, defeating mid-air enemies that attempt to twist and pervert the things that you say and do. Say things like, "Michael. I need those in your authority to come and fight this battle for the Kingdom of God's sake. The Bible said that you were able to defeat Satan's army, bind him, and throw him into a pit. I need you to send angelic allies now to (accomplish whichever specific task needs to be accomplished)." In other instances where you need messages sent, you can say, "Gabriel. The Bible shows you expediently sending messages of comfort, peace, and assurance to people under God's authority. It also says that the words of the wise can be used for healing and blessing. I ask you now to send angels within your authority to send this message of (message description) to (person's name or description) right now".

The Story Of Gloria And Her Angelic Encounter

A lady named Gloria told her story of her angelic alliance. She said that she was helping her son move from Wisconsin to Washington DC (approximately 14 hours). She drove with her daughter. They left her son at night for their hotel nearby in Maryland. She described her menopausal misery saying that she was having hot flashes so bad that she felt hot even when the air condition was making her daughter feel cold, so she decided to take a shower, then she tried to fall back to sleep. She started to feel tugging at her blankets so she opened her eyes. She said:

I opened my eyes and saw a bright being, all dressed in white. It's arms were extended and it was pulling the blankets up around me. I saw it's eyes, but couldn't make out any face features. It was like I had to put on my glasses, because everything was blurry. (But I don't wear glasses.) And I saw yellow, where the hair should be on it's head.

The first thing I did was jerk up to my elbows and I wanted to scream. It said, "It's alright. I'm covering you. Don't be afraid." Then it looked over it's left shoulder, toward my daughter's bed, with her puppy and looked back at me and said, "You don't want to wake anyone up." For some reason, I thought it must be one of my daughters. They both have blonde hair,..and hey, it MUST be one of my daughters. I felt so peaceful. My heart had been breaking and now I had such comfort. I felt like a child all over again.

It said then, "Go to sleep, I'm tucking you in."

So I closed my eyes, and could feel the quilts being tucked in around me. I had no fear and great peace. I remember laughing as I was falling asleep, because I thought, "Boy,...I must have looked a fright."[2]

Angels Respond To Our Slightest Discomfort

Angels respond to our slightest discomfort because they are submitted to an authority who cares about the minutest detail of our lives. Our King knows the number of hairs on our head, and He desires for us to be able to reach our highest potential in life. Open your mind to the idea that you are not limited in your flesh because you have supernatural alliances when you focus on your limitless spiritual abilities.

Every ministry or church has an angel-the angel of the ministry or of the covenant upon which the ministry is established. In Revelation 2-3, you see God giving rebuke or instruction to a certain church through the instrumentality of the angel of that church. In this, we can know that not only do individuals have angels assigned, but ministries, and larger bodies of people have angels assigned as well. Your ministry has an angel, ask God to make it known to you and then seek to develop this friendship and partnership in your ministry. When any ministry is born on earth, it is first birthed in the realm of the spirit. The Lord raises an altar in the realm of the spirit with fire burning on it and an angel is assigned to keep that fire burning. That is the angel of the ministry. It is this angel that goes into bringing the supply of that ministry. In partnership with the Holy Spirit, that angel runs the

[2] http://www.angelslight.org/angelstory.php?id=gloria

spiritual operations of that ministry.

You can communicate to your angel thru spoken or written words, arts, and expressions. In addition to your ability thru your alliance with Michael, Gabriel, and the angels that stand guard for you and your ministry, you can also develop a relationship with the angels standing watch over people or congregations who present opposition to the Kingdom of God being manifested thru you.

Learn To Identify Godly Inspiration Vs. Evil Inspiration

Galatians 5:14-26 tells us the behaviors that we can observe when a person is submitted to their flesh or when a person is oppressed or possessed by demonic spirits. This passage also tell us about behaviors of those who are submitted to the spirit of God. It says:

"For the entire law is fulfilled in keeping this one command: "Love your neighbor as yourself." If you bite and devour each other, watch out or you will be destroyed by each other.

So I say, walk by the Spirit, and you will not gratify the desires of the flesh. For the flesh desires what is contrary to the Spirit, and the Spirit what is contrary to the flesh. They are in conflict with each other, so that you are not to do whatever you want. But if you are led by the Spirit, you are not under the law.

The acts of the flesh are obvious: sexual immorality, impurity and debauchery; idolatry and witchcraft; hatred, discord, jealousy, fits of rage, selfish ambition, dissensions, factions and envy; drunkenness, orgies, and the like. I warn you, as I did before, that those who live like this will not inherit the kingdom of God. But the fruit of the Spirit is love, joy, peace, forbearance, kindness, goodness, faithfulness, gentleness and self-control. Against such things there is no law. Those who belong to Christ Jesus have crucified the flesh with its passions and desires. Since we live by the Spirit, let us keep in step with the Spirit. Let us not become conceited, provoking and envying each other."

With this, we know that if a person is manifesting fruits of the flesh, we can communicate with their angel to advocate for that person's spirit. You can say, "Angel who stands watch for (person's name), you and I see this person manifesting the fruits of the flesh, and submitting to the forces of evil. The Bible says that people who are submitted to the authorities of darkness will not enter the Kingdom of God. You and I both want (person's name) to enter into Heaven eternally. Right now, I petition you before the throne of Heaven to gather the Heavenly army, and fight to restore (person's name) to their rightful place in the Kingdom of God. I give you authority to attack all of the demons who have access to this person's life. I cancel any contracts that they might have and I deny them access now."

Summary

- Be aware of the spiritual
- Develop a relationship with the angels
- Understand their hierarchy and roles
- Study their history
- Invite their partnership in your ministry

CHAPTER ELEVEN

DENY EVIL ACCESS

"Spiritual warfare is very real. There is a furious, fierce, and fero-
cious battle raging in the realm of the spirit between the forces
of God and the forces of evil. Warfare happens every day, all the
time. Whether you believe it or not, you are in a battlefield. You
are in warfare."

— Pedro Okoro

The Story Of Dennis

D ennis was a very spiritual young boy. He was practicing
witchcraft. The spirits that he prayed to would instruct
him of where to find money, how to attain it, and how to
ruin those around him that make him feel uncomfortable. He was
only 16 years old and living with his parents when he began this
spiritual lifestyle. His parents became completely overwhelmed:
their belongings would come up missing, their money unaccount-
ed for, and their son became very isolated, destructive, and sneaky.

He has been known to be affiliated with a girl who lost her hair
after making Dennis upset. His math teacher had given him an
"F" in the class for not turning in assignments. On his way home,
Dennis stood on the side of the road, holding up a spiritually-affiliated hand signal, and the teacher got into a fatal car accident as
a result. Many students and teachers have complained about his

spiritually-affiliated behaviors that cause harm to the students and teachers. As a result, the teachers at school dismissed him from their classroom for their feelings that he is affiliated with disruptive behavior and harmful attacks against other students.

On one occasion, Dennis's parents walked into his room unannounced, and saw him praying to a demonic spirit, slicing his wrist in exchange for something that he wanted. He was yelling, "I am pouring out my blood to you. Just give me what I have asked you for!"

They know that he is worshipping some alternative spirit, but they are unsure of who. They take him to church weekly, but he does not take that seriously because he says, "They just do some drama with no signs or results". When the pastor and ministers pray, they rebuke and shout, but nothing seems to change for Dennis.

How The Kingdom Of Darkness Affects The World

In the books of Genesis and Revelations, the Bible shows that some of the angels had fallen and become apart of the kingdom of darkness. In Genesis, they fell for preying on beautiful women, and formed a mixed (half-human and half-angel) breed called nephilim. The nephilim became fierce tribes of people that fought against God's chosen people on many occasions. On another occasion, in Revelations, the angels were thrown from Heaven for following Satan in his rebellious acts.

Mixed breeds (half-human and half-angel) still exist today. The result of the angels being thrown from Heaven to Earth (in Revelations) heavily populated our space; creating an Earth that is more heavily populated in the air than in the flesh. Even the seas are populated by fallen angels, and they are preying on people; trying to find a platform for mischief to leave hell inhabited. Typically, a person becomes a mixed breed thru choices made in ignorance that invite the fallen angel to inhabit their body. Choices such a sex outside of marriage, listening to music that opposes the laws of God, entertaining ill behavior, and unfortunately, by way of transmutation, you can also be born into a family that has invited their presence. Today, the mixed breed of fallen angel and human is called demon possession.

When a person is demon possessed, they experience a loss of control and demonstrate the fruits of the flesh: sexual immorality, impurity and debauchery; idolatry and witchcraft; hatred, discord, jealousy, fits of rage, selfish ambition, dissensions, factions and envy; drunkenness, orgies, and the like.

You Are The Target Market For The Kingdom Of Darkness

Potential is the target for the kingdom of darkness. When they see someone with substantial potential to take territory from them or to increase the number of those that inhabit the Kingdom of Heaven, they charge at the person with temptations that they believe would hinder them from success. Because of their insight, they have taken advantage of many people and they target those that man believes are the least likely to fall (like our present and future leaders). They have the ability to gain insight into the future. The kingdom of darkness has the ability to target lineage based on how they believe God has appointed them. For this reason, the Israelites experienced a lot of turmoil because thru their lineage lied the seed (Jesus) and plan of salvation (the gospel) for the whole world. Demon possession is very common, but children and marriages are an increased target for the kingdom of darkness.

In married couples, demon possession causes a disruption in their unity and stunts their sex life. Rather than having sex as an expression of love, couples that experience torment from demon possession are being plagued by temptation to accept pornographic habits, adultery, sex with animals, swinging/open marriages, homosexual attraction, or avoiding sex entirely. When successful, the kingdom of darkness can cause a marriage to greatly affect many people thru their children, their mentorees, and all those that are around them. It can be poisonous!

Children become victims of demon possession by way of immature exposure to things that have conditions. When children are exposed to sex prematurely, demons can inhabit them with ease; for this reason rape, molestation, and other forcible attacks with sex are common tools used by the kingdom of darkness to steal dreams or the child's feeling of access to their dreams. Demons can also be granted access to children by other poor choices of the parents. When the parents allow the exposure of their children, it is like signing an agreement and surrendering the keys to the destiny of your generations.

Say, "No!" to the enemy

There are many people with a thorough understanding of the spiritual world, and that can be for your good or bad. Some people, like Dennis have opened lines of communication with forces of evil that mean you and others harm. They have opened these lines of communication because they believe that the spiritual consultation that they are receiving is for their good. These forces require your consciousness in prayer in order to avoid them from being a menace and terrorizing with the intent of killing you and your loved ones. People naively entertain demonic forces because they have believed the lie that they can offer them any good.

Jesus said, "The thief comes only to steal and kill and destroy; I have come that they may have life, and have it to the full." The kingdom of darkness desires your eternal damnation, therefore, you must fight them with no pity or compassion as they do to you. They are the only force that inspires hatred and feel an advantage by seeing your eternal failure to hell. Flesh and blood (mankind) may respond submissively to the kingdom of darkness (which is a wrong unbiblical choice), but you must understand that if you do not fight back spiritually by binding and canceling the contracts and authority of Satan, then you are fighting monotonously and in vain. For this reason, Paul said in Ephesians 6:12, "For our struggle is not against flesh and blood, but against the rulers, against the authorities, against the powers of this dark world and against the spiritual forces of evil in the Heavenly realms." You NEED to learn to fight against the kingdom of darkness in prayer, otherwise, you will be bullied around; having life trial and tribulation after another until death!

Say, "No! I do not believe. I do not receive!" Just as real as are angels and their work and operations, so also are demons. The air around us you is infested with malevolent forces who seek to destroy your effectiveness and fellowship with God. Sometimes they come against you with discouragement, overwhelming suggestions and thoughts of complacency, stagnancy, defeat, inabilities, and weakness. But it is for you to discern truth, and never to accept them by aligning your talk with them.

Even though you are overwhelmed with negative thoughts, it is as your responses to them that gives consent to the devil to bring them to pass in your life. If you do not agree with the devil and respond accordingly, he can not work those negative things out in your life. What are you supposed to do when Satan brings those evil suggestions to you? Say "No! I refuse to believe and I will never receive it." If he brings them a hundred times, you counter it a hundred and ten times.

"Death and life are in the power of the tongue, and those who love it shall eat the fruit thereof." The spiritual realm acts by the consent of your words. You see your thoughts, actions, and words are the deciding factors in your victory or defeat in the battles of life with demons and Satan. They are the most potent tools and weapons that you ever need in spiritual dealings. In a bid to be able to handle the devil and his schemes, you have have to have knowledge and understanding of your God, His word, your power, and your allies to defeat him.

Get familiar with the kingdom of darkness

My people are destroyed for lack of knowledge the Bible says. (Hosea 4:6).The things that you don't know kill faster than the things you know. The HIV virus can be managed if you know about it. But if you don't, death, imminent and incipient death will be the result. In the realm of the spirit, the gravest danger is ignorance. In short, the Bible likens ignorance to darkness. Where there is ignorance, the devil is chief.

Some feel that if you leave Satan alone, he will leave you alone. This fear is from Satan himself, and it is meant for your destruction. You cannot believe that if you leave Satan alone that he will leave you alone! This is not true! Satan, being a prince of darkness works unhindered where he is not known, talked or taught about. Get to know your enemy.

Understand the hierarchy

Just like the angels of God are in hierarchy, so also is the kingdom of Satan. He sits as chief over his kingdom of darkness and appoints rulers and sub rulers under him to help carry out his wicked acts.

The Bible gave us information about the hierarchy of his government in Ephesians 6:12. They are:

Principalities Or Rulers

These are princes of darkness in charge of certain satanic regions and zones. They are the chieftain in the hierarchy of the demonic kingdom, next to Satan himself. reformersrecovery.com said, "The word principality comes from the greek word arche where we get are words like archduke, or archbishop. A principality can be a word for a princes territory these demons are similar to Archangels in God's hierarchy. Because these demons are linked with the geopolitical term princes territory these demons are believed to be political in nature. Everything divisive between nations whether building nuclear weapons, or funding terrorist is spurred on by principalities".

The work of a principality was demonstrated in Daniel 10:12-13 in response to Daniel's prayers for his people to be brought out of bondage in Babylon. An angel came to Daniel and said,

"Do not be afraid, Daniel. Since the first day that you set your mind to gain understanding and to humble yourself before your God, your words were heard, and I have come in response to them. But the prince of the Persian kingdom resisted me twenty-one days. Then Michael, one of the chief princes, came to help me, because I was detained there with the king of Persia. Now I have come to explain to you what will happen to your people in the future, for the vision concerns a time yet to come."

The "prince of the Persian kingdom" was a principality in charge of creating division in a region. Principalities still operate to create division in our world today; creating confusion between governments and people.

Powers And Spiritual Hosts Of Wickedness In Heavenly Places

Similar to the angelic hierarchy that appoints a guardian angel to each human, the kingdom of darkness has assigned a hierarchy of demons from nation to family to individuals. These demon spirits sit over certain operations of Satan's kingdom. Their advantage is their insight of your individual and family temptations and falls. They use this insight to plot against people and lead them away from God.

Regarding rulers of the darkness of this age, reformersministry.org said, "This phrase in the original is actually one word kosmokratopas which literally means world rulers of the darkness of this age. In the Bible the word Kosmos translated word is often used to refer the the world system. Which is to say the prevailing thought, customs, or philosophy amongst unbelievers this is in distinction to God's kingdom which operates on different philosophies." Rulers of the darkness of this age operate by distributing philosophical ideas that oppose the Bible. Evolution, atheism, agnosticism, philosophies that suggest human sovereignty apart from God, accepted evils, and the like are works of the rulers of the darkness of this age.

Spiritual hosts of wickedness in the Heavenly places are tasked with deterring people from the Spirit of God by providing something that appears like it. Cults, false religions, pluralism, false doctrine, division, people who act like christians, complacency, and fear all imitate the spiritual connectedness that can be achieved thru prayer, connectedness with God, and a connection with a body of believers such as the church.

These are four major hierarchical divisions of the kingdom of Satan. Some of these demons are over continents, some over nations, some over cities and communities and over individuals, all carrying out the evil intent of Satan upon the human creation.

Know Your Armor

Equally important to having a workable knowledge of the kingdom of darkness is the knowledge of the armor; the protective and offensive weapons that God has given us to frustrate the devils affront upon us.

They are listed by the apostle in Ephesians 6, where he told us of Satan and his operational hierarchy also. They are:

- The belt of truth for the waist
- The breastplate of righteousness for the chest

- The shoes called peace, for your feet
- The faith shield, to block off satanic arrows, our protective cover.
- The helmet called salvation, for our mind.
- The sword-which is God's word, for offense
- Prayer and watchfulness

I discuss the armor of God in greater length in my book, 12 Undeniable Laws For Being A Kingdom of Heaven Ambassador. With all these weapons in place, we can be sure to bring down the devil and his tantrums and also assault his kingdom in return. We don't just stay in the defensive but also we can gain an offensive advantage against him. In the military, offense is a better strategy than defense.

(See Ephesians 6:13-18)

Master the Art of War

What is the use of having this entire set of weaponry and not knowing how to use them? So we must put on every piece of the armor, wearing them in their proper place; righteousness for the breast and chest, helmet for the head, belt for the waist, shield on the left hand and the sword on the right hand, peace as shoes on the feet and having done all, be ready to do battle. Stand therefore ....

Summary

- Deny evil access.
- Say, "No! I do not believe. I do not receive!"
- Get familiar with the Kingdom of Darkness
- Understand the hierarchy
- Know Your Armor
- Master the Art of War

CHAPTER TWELVE

RECORD REVELATIONS

"A single dream is more powerful than a thousand realities."

— J.R.R. Tolkien

The Story Of Ramona

Ramona was a dreamer. At times, she would have dreams that would wake her out of her sleep, but because she did not have a solution, she was not able to sleep afterwards. She felt disrupted by the dreams for years. She would see people in the split second prior to a car accident or a person holding a gun to his head, and it would frighten her. As a child, Ramona's mother would say, "Go back to sleep! Ignore that craziness!". Ramona thought that it was a personal problem or a curse that she would have frequent dreams, so she kept it a secret.

In her early 20's, she stayed with a friend for a four month stint. Her friend was a night hawk and was most productive in the late night/very early hours of the day; when Ramona would wake from her dreams. With her friend being awake, Ramona decided to confide in her, and share about her tragic dreams. Ramona's friend was a spiritual woman and had some understanding about revelation. When Ramona told her friend about these odd dreams, her friend told her, "You need to write those visions down and pray to God for understanding! The Bible always used dreams as a warning of a future circumstance. It sounds like God is assigning you to intercede for some specific people".

Ramona began to record her dreams, she would wake up and intercede for those that she saw, and she would pray for understanding. After her prayer (sometimes during), she would fall back into a deep sleep, and she started feeling more rejuvenated. God was showing her the people that she was assigned to; sometimes on television, sometimes in government, some were family, some friends, and others were perfect strangers. She started seeing the fruits of her role. People that she was praying for were testifying about almost being in a car crash, but hearing a voice or angel that interceded. She had people come to her that were suicidal and heard a voice that caused them to spare their lives, she saw sick people healed, and many other miraculous things began to happen around her when she began to record her revelations, intercede for those that she saw, and ask God for understanding.

The Importance Of Dreams

One third of your life is spent sleeping. The Bible tells us numerous stories where God counseled men in their dreams, thru prophesy, or in a midday trance. Revelations from God have been used to inspire, save nations, prevent suicides, give hope, make destinies known, and grant many more successes to mankind. Unfortunately, today many people do not understand the importance of dreams and God's coordination with man, therefore, they miss out on the insight that can restore their wholeness and the wholeness of those around them.

The greatest book in the world, the Bible, has been a staple for mankind for centuries because some men took the steps to write down what God said to them. The Bible is a record of God's relation with the human people beginning with the creation of the Heavens and the earth, and foretelling the present and future plans of God for man. This dealing with man came in the form of vision, revelation, dreams, manifestations, prophecies, and the like. We have the Bible because somebody wrote down their revelation from God.

The authors of the Bible wrote what they heard and saw. Whether it was the direct voice of God that they heard, an angel that spoke to them, a dream that they had, or a vision that they saw, they wrote down their revelations. Even the account of Christ's dealing with Satan is written in the Bible!

For short, the Bible in your hands because somebody heard God in a dream, vision, prophesy, audible voice, or revelation, and wrote it down. It is therefore important that you write down God's dealing with you. Whether they be visions, dreams, petitions, prophesy, manifestation, or any other way, God has been revealing Himself to you. Write it down! God can reveals secret insight about life, ministry, marriage, and business through dreams, visions, and prophecy. Regarding the importance of recording God's dealing with you, the Bible says:

"I am the Alpha and the Omega, the First and the Last," and, "What you see, write in a book ... "I am He who lives, and was dead, and behold, I am alive forevermore. Amen. And I have the keys of Hades and of Death. "Write the things which you have seen, and the things which are, and the things which will take place after this. (Revelation 1:11-19)

Oh, that my words were written! Oh, that they were inscribed in a book! (Job 19:23)

I personally did not understand the power of revelation until meeting my husband in 2010. I had very vivid dreams, but not on a regular basis. No one in my environment had ever spoken about the importance of dreams. In response to my childhood dreams, my mom would comfort me, and help me to get back to sleep. Our family did not know how important our nightly dreams were, so we tried ignoring them and returning to sleep.

On one occasion, (within one month of meeting my husband) I had a very shocking dream that made me wake up crying, and it compelled me to speak to my husband about dreams. I said, "I keep having crazy dreams that are waking me up from my sleep." His advice to me was to write it down, ask God for understanding, and keep a record as God reveals the meaning.

Following our conversation, my husband and I studied the Bible regarding dreams, so that I could understand their importance and their potential application in my life. We paid special attention to the fact that the Bible mentions those that were proponents of relationship with the God of Heaven (like Abraham, Isaac, Jacob, Moses, Daniel, David, Solomon, and many more), and those that were opponents to the people of God (such as King Nebuchadnezzar and The Pharoah of Egypt), and how both highly valued the revelation from God.

One year later, when I was one month away from getting on a plane to Africa to marry my husband, I asked God in my heart for His confirmation that I was fulfilling His assignment for me thru marriage. On a returning flight from my brother's funeral, a Haitian lady sat next to me on the plane. We did not know one another (not even names). She began telling me that my trip to Africa would be a success. I will have a lot of fun, and the man that I would marry is a gift from God and a pastor. She began telling me that I should expect children as God's gift to me. I was confident that God had used her to speak a message of assurance to me. Her prophecy was confirmation to me that I was pursuing a path that would please God.

How To Distinguish The Author Of Your Revelation

The authors of revelation can inhabit either the Kingdom or Heaven or the kingdom of darkness. God and the angels or Satan and his demons can communicate with you thru dreams, visions, audible voices, and other forms of revelation, so you must be careful of what you entertain, and discern whether the dream inspired deeds that would give you life or deeds that would culminate and bring you death.

The kingdom of darkness uses revelation to plant lies, to inspire evil, to invoke idolatry, and to decrease your sensitivity to love and the things of God. Demons veil themselves and attempt to participate with you in many evils. They can inspire your praises for material things or people. The kingdom of darkness can have sex with men and women in their dreams, overwhelm their minds with pornographic images, inspire bad habits, and reinforce negative words and treatment. What you have listened to or watched throughout the day can become the subject of your dreams, therefore you should be careful with what you entertain because it can be twisted, altered, or even used to torment you in your sleep.

When the kingdom of Heaven is the author of a revelation, it is used to warn, rebuke, encourage, or empower. You may receive supernatural ideas, new inventions, increased creativity, warnings that can save or transform lives, messages that guide, assurance, and so much more.

The Story Of Tanya - The Hard-working Woman

Tanya was a hardworking woman. She had been working full-time, going to nursing school, and doing her clinical training alongside it all. She kept having a horrific dream every night, but because she woke up every morning rushing to work, she interrupted the dream on every occurrence, and never remembered or understood it entirely. She started to manifest sickness in her body, her doctor diagnosed her with walking pneumonia, and told her that she should stay home for two weeks of recovery time.

In her recovery time, Tanya had the recurring dream. She saw children in a beautiful garden, they were raising their hands, and waiting on her to call on them. They were referring to her as "Teacher". In her dream, even the adults were raising their hands, and listening for insight.

The next night, she had a dream. In the dream, she was holding a certificate and crying. She had lost her house, her car, and her family was fighting.

When she woke up, she inquired of God saying, "Father, bring understanding to me now". She wrote down the key action, which was that she was in school close to receiving her nursing certificate, but graduating would not make her happy. Her family is already in an uproar, and it seems to get worse as she continues in school. The key emotion was sadness.

She recalled the earlier dream. In that, the key action was that she was teaching. The key emotion was enjoyment. She started to think about how her present life was such a burden, and she has not had joy with it for awhile. She recognized that she was in nursing school for the projected income rather than fulfillment. Tanya realized that God wants her to teach, but she knew that it was in a non-traditional way because her dream took place in a garden.

Tanya prayed to God saying, "Father, you are almighty. You created me and assigned me here for a purpose, and I can see you speaking to me thru my dream. I ask you now that you would guide the way to the place where I can reach my highest potential now".

The next day when Tanya was at work, a co-worker came into her office and complemented her plants. This had happened many times before, but this time the person seemed so genuine and thoroughly concerned saying, "God has given you a gift. Not everyone has a passion like this for plant life as to fill up their office with plants and come in daily to maintain them. I see that your schedule is extremely busy, so you must see great importance in maintaining the plants in your office, otherwise they would have all died. I think you should start a nursery or something. I would buy from you!"

Tanya had an "aha" moment. She remembered her childhood dream of owning a botanical garden and nursery. She understood what God was trying to tell her in the dream. She switched her major in school from nursing to horticulture sciences, she went to a local nursery, and stocked up on seedlings. Tanya began by planting 500 plants and reinvested her profits. Within two years, she was able to have deja vu as she sat in front of an audience of

100 people (children and adults) teaching a gardening class that she was hosting at her own nursery.

Keys To Dream Interpretation

On "It's Supernatural! with Sid Roth, Mark Virkler said that rather than going to books and attempting to interpret the symbols of dreams, we should inquire about what the symbols actually mean to us. He said that in Genesis, when Joseph dreamed, he had agricultural symbols (husks of corn and cattle) that had meaning to him. Similarly, Nebuchadnezzar saw a golden statue that was cut down in his dream. The golden statue had meaning to Nebuchadnezzar that it would not have to you. You cannot explain things as subjective and customized as God's coordination with you thru a book or video that promises to interpret normal symbols. Like Tanya, you should ask God to give you understanding, investigate the key action that was requested of you in the dream and the key emotion that was attached to it, and be open for God to interpret the dream to you thru His audible voice, his prophets, future dreams, trances, meditation, or in prayer.

Some dreams are startling and tell us how we can secure success rather than tragedy in our futures. The first thing to understand when you awake startled from a dream is that God reveals to redeem. He does not reveal to invoke fear, but fear is our typical response. Job 33:13-18 says, "For God does speak—now one way, now another— though no one perceives it. In a dream, in a vision of the night, when deep sleep falls on people as they slumber in their beds, he may speak in their ears and terrify them with warnings, to turn them from wrongdoing and keep them from pride, to preserve them from the pit, their lives from perishing by the sword." Understand that the startling dreams (when they are not distortions of what we put into our minds) are usually warnings to us. When you do not understand the meaning, write it down, and inquire of God, saying, "Father, give me understanding of what you have just shown me."

Dreams, visions, and revelation can:

- Transform generations

- Leave a legacy

- Warn Nations, Large bodies of people, or warn you specifically of future events (good or bad)

- Show you how to tweak your actions for maximum success

Write your dreams down! Talk to God and request understanding when you do not understand it, and allow your dreams, visions, and revelations to transform your life!

Summary

- Revelation is important

- Take your revelations seriously

- Distinguish the author of your revelation

- Know that revelation is customized to you, so you must seek God for interpretation

DIVINE COMMISSION FOR PRAYER

Now I admonish you to guard your prayers with diligence, for out of your prayers flow the grace and power of God. You guard your prayers by watching your words and your thanksgiving.

Once you have prayed, God has heard you, so start thanking God for the image that you see prior to the answer. Thank Him for the process and for the answers. You will see the answer to your prayer materialize. Anytime, your petition comes to your mind, just say, "Lord, I thank you because you have heard me and I know you hear me always". The answer will come. You have protected your prayer.

You cannot pray about a particular issue and leave God's presence still talking as if what you prayed for is not done. Even when it has not happened, believe that God has heard you, and start to see and to declare what God has said about it.

In Mark 11:24 Jesus said, "Whatsoever you desire, when you pray, believe that you have received it and you shall have." You received it at the instance of praying. You received it the moment you say in the Jesus name and conclude the prayer. But before the actual manifestation, the waiting time, you have got to watch what you say about it; otherwise, you would destroy the prayer you have said. So many times we go into God's presence and pray, but the moment we are out of that place, we start talking and living as if we have never prayed; the confession of our mouth just goes contrary to the prayer we have just said. We just begin to unsay what we have said. In that way, we have not protected our prayer.

An affirmation to repeat in times where you need to renew your faith as you are waiting on your answer:

Now, Lord, my God, you have made your servant an ambassador of your Kingdom. Give me a patient and submitted heart to maintain my faith and hope as I wait on the answer of my prayer that has not yet materialized. I ask that you would free any angels that may be struggling to bring me my answer. I deny evil access from deterring the answer to my prayer. I open my eyes and ears for Heavenly revelation now, and I resubmit my petition before you in the name of Jesus Christ of Nazareth!

If you know a scripture that says, "If you do …, then I will do", ensure that you are maintaining your part of the condition to receive the promise, and include that in your prayer. May God continue to increase your wisdom in the area of prayer in Jesus name.

-Tiffany Domena

ABOUT THE AUTHOR

Tiffany Domena is an Ambassador of the Kingdom of Heaven, wife, mother, bestselling author, and advocate for living your life by YHWH's design. Bringing nine years of military experience, an educational background in Bible (Bachelor's in Religion along with some graduate coursework), and a Biblical worldview, Tiffany enjoys training others on how to be successful in their deployments to the Earth. She is the founder at Kingdom of Heaven Ambassadors International where her primary focus is taking enemy territory back on the internet and in mainstream media, and refocusing hearts and minds on Yeshua the Messiah. Expertly publishing ten books, hosting a podcast, and blogging on pertinent topics that strike our world, Tiffany's passion bleeds thru her work, and encourages those who get wind of her. She has been known to speak and write on topics including prayer, life purpose, marriage, sex, temptation, goal-setting, wisdom, and prosperity. Other books by Tiffany include:

12 Undeniable Laws For Prosperity

12 Undeniable Laws For Being A Kingdom of Heaven Ambassador

12 Undeniable Laws For Sex

12 Undeniable Laws For Marriage

12 Undeniable Laws For Being Wise As A Snake

Perception: The World's Most Affluent Leader and companion workbook

Transform Your Habits To Create Your Position of Power Workbook

Someone Covets You

Find more resources, training, or to subscribe to Tiffany's blog, podcast, or social network, visit www.kingdomofheavenambassador.com.

ONE LAST THING...

If you enjoyed this book, I would love to hear! I personally read all reviews written on my books, and I use them to make the books better and more effective. I would greatly appreciate your feedback at the links below:

Amazon Link:

http://www.amazon.com/Tiffany-Domena/e/B00MSHE0LI

Website Link:

http://www.kingdomofheavenambassador.com/shop/

Goodreads Link:

https://www.goodreads.com/author/show/8459952.
Tiffany_Domena

May God bless you!

Tiffany Domena

www.ingramcontent.com/pod-product-compliance
Lightning Source LLC
LaVergne TN
LVHW021342080426
835508LV00020B/2083